Plot, Chapters, Scenes, Beats

Plot, Chapters, Scenes, Beats:

Everything You Need to Start Writing Your Novel

By Ross Samsky

MZP Studio

Plot, Chapters, Scenes, Beats: Everything you Need to Start Writing Your Novel

No part of this publication may be reproduced, stored in a retrieval system, or transmitted in any form or by any means — electronic, mechanical, photocopying, recording, or otherwise — without the prior written permission of the author, except for brief quotations used in reviews or critical articles.

This book is a work of nonfiction. While every effort has been made to ensure accuracy, the author makes no warranties regarding the content and accepts no liability for any loss or damage resulting from the use of the information contained herein.

Published by MZP Studio

United States of America

ISBN: 979-8-9940000-8-3

First Edition

Cover design by Ross Samsky

Interior design by Ross Samsky

Printed in the United States of America

Foreword

Writing a novel is often described as a mysterious process, something reserved for people with rare talent or sudden inspiration. In reality, the only difference between those who finish a novel and those who never begin is structure. A story becomes manageable when you understand how it works. The steps become clearer. The blank page becomes less intimidating. What once felt unreachable becomes something you can build.

This workbook exists to give you that structure. It does not promise shortcuts, nor does it suggest that writing is effortless. Instead, it provides a practical, repeatable method that turns the complex task of writing a novel into a series of small, achievable actions. You will not be asked to rely on luck or wait for motivation. You will learn how to create a solid foundation, build your story layer by layer, and understand what each part of a novel must accomplish.

The pages ahead are designed for any writer, at any stage. Whether you have a clear idea or only a faint spark, you will find a path you can follow. Every exercise invites you to think, experiment, and shape the material in a way that reflects your voice and your goals. You will construct your plot, develop your chapters, craft your scenes, and break them down into beats that drive your story forward. By the time you reach the end, you will not just understand how novels work. You will have the blueprint for yourself.

Writing a novel is not a matter of waiting for inspiration. It is a matter of building steadily, thinking clearly, and trusting the process. This workbook will guide you through that process with clarity and practicality. All you need to bring is your willingness to begin and the persistence to keep going.

If you do that, the story you want to tell will take shape. The tools are here. The guidance is here. And the next page is where your novel truly starts.

- Ross Samsky

Table of Contents

Introduction 1

How to Use This "Workbook" 3

Choosing Your Path Through This Book 4

Step 1: Understanding Plot Structures 5

   The Three Act Structure 5

      The Hero's Journey 6

      Save the Cat Beat Sheet 7

      Freytag's Pyramid 7

      The Seven Point Plot Structure 8

      Step 1A: The Three Act Structure – A Deeper Understanding 10

      Step 1B: The Hero's Journey – A Deeper Understanding 12

      Step 1C: Save the Cat Beat Sheet – A Deeper Understanding 16

      Step 1D: Freytag's Pyramid – A Deeper Understanding 20

      Step 1E: The Seven Point Plot Structure – A Deeper Understanding 22

      Activity Step 1: Choosing Your Plot Structure 25

   Step 2: Understanding Chapters 26

      Step 2A: Chapters in the Three Act Structure 26

      Step 2B: Chapters in the Hero's Journey 30

      Step 2C: Chapters in Save the Cat 37

      Step 2D: Chapters in Freytag's Pyramid 43

      Step 2E: Chapters in the Seven Point Plot Structure 46

      Activity Step 2: Expanding Your Plot Points into Chapters 50

   Step 3: Understanding Scenes *51*

      Step 3A: Scenes in the Three Act Structure 53

Step 3B: Scenes in the Hero's Journey 64
Step 3C: Scenes in Save the Cat 73
Step 3D: Scenes in Freytag's Pyramid.. 81
Step 3E: Scenes in the Seven Point Plot Structure 89
Activity Step 3: Adding Scenes to Your Chapters 94

Step 4: Understanding Beats..95

Step 4A: Beats in the Three Act Structure... 97
Step 4B: Beats in the Hero's Journey 104
Step 4C: Beats in Save the Cat 110
Step 4D: Beats in Freytag's Pyramid 116
Step 4E: Beats in the Seven Point Plot Structure.................................... 121
Activity for Step 4: Breaking Scenes into Beats 124

Step 5: Turning Your Structure Into Story 125

Index: Generic Samples 132

3 ACT STRUCTURE — STANDARD CHAPTER, SCENE AND BEAT OUTLINE 132

HERO'S JOURNEY PLOT LINE.. 138

SAVE THE CAT — OFFICIAL 15 BEATS WITH SCENES + BEATS 143

FREYTAG'S PYRAMID —STRUCTURE WITH CHAPTERS, SCENES AND BEATS 148

SEVEN POINT PLOT STRUCTURE — FULL CHAPTER, SCENE, AND BEAT OUTLINE 153

Introduction

Writing a novel often feels mysterious until someone finally lays out the steps in plain, workable terms. This workbook is designed to do exactly that. Think of it as a guided path rather than a strict rulebook. You will walk through each stage of building a story from the ground up and shape your own ideas as you go. Whether you have been circling the dream of writing a novel for years or you only recently felt the spark, you will find a structure here that removes the guesswork and helps you focus on the creative work that matters.

You do not need experience. You do not need the perfect idea. You only need a willingness to show up and put words on the page. Everything else can be learned, and this workbook will show you how to break a novel into clear, manageable parts. Let us begin at the foundation.

Every novel, no matter the genre or style, follows a simple hierarchy. A story is built from a plot, which is divided into chapters, which are made of scenes, which are formed from beats. Once you understand how these layers work together, the process stops from feeling overwhelming. You no longer face a blank void. You face a series of small, achievable steps.

This workbook will guide you through each layer. You will learn what a plot is, how common structures work, and how to shape your own. You will learn how chapters function, what scenes accomplish, and how beats carry the emotional and narrative weight of every moment. You will also find space to explore your own ideas, since no two writers will use this material in the same way.

The goal is clarity. By the end, you will know how to take a concept and turn it into a structured outline that can support a full novel. You will also have a stronger sense of what makes stories work and how to apply those principles to your own writing.

Take your time. Move at your own pace. Use the pages to experiment, revise, and discover. This is your process, and this workbook is here to help you shape it into something real.

A novel is built in layers. When you break those layers down, the structure becomes much easier to understand. It begins with the plot. The plot is divided into chapters. Each chapter contains scenes. Each scene is made of beats. Some writers go even smaller and divide beats into atomic or micro beats. Seeing the story arranged this way helps you focus on one level at a time instead of feeling overwhelmed by the full scope of the book.

Each layer has its own purpose. The plot is the complete journey of your story from start to finish. Chapters break that journey into major steps that guide the reader forward. Scenes show events unfolding in real time and reveal character growth or important information. Beats create the moment-to-moment movement inside a scene through action, reaction, or emotional change. Atomic beats capture the smallest shifts, such as a pause, a glance, or a change in tone. Together, these layers give your novel structure and make the writing process more manageable.

Structure Overview Diagram

Plot
→ Chapters
→ Scenes
→ Beats
→ Atomic or Micro Beats

Plot
The full journey of the story. It covers what the protagonist wants, the challenges ahead, and how everything resolves.

Chapters
Major sections of the story. Each one handles a meaningful step forward, a shift in direction, or a change in the character's situation.

Scenes
Real-time events that take place within a chapter. A scene shows something happening that moves the story or develops the character.

Beats
Smaller moments inside a scene. Each beat marks an action, reaction, choice, or emotional change.

How to Use This "Workbook"

This workbook is a guide, not a place to write your novel. You will follow the steps here while doing all of your actual writing in a separate notebook, journal, word processor, tablet app, or any other medium.

As you move through each step, keep this workbook open on your device and keep your writing tool beside you. When you see an Activity section, pause and complete the work in your own document. Do not worry about formatting or perfection. Your only job is to think on the page and follow the structure you have built.

You can reread any section as often as you like. Use the Table of Contents to jump directly to the plot structure or step you are currently working on.

Choosing Your Path Through This Book

This book is designed so you can follow it step by step from beginning to end. If you are new to plot structure or you want to build your novel from the ground up, start with Step 1 and continue forward in order.

If you already know which plot structure you plan to use—such as the Hero's Journey, Save the Cat, Freytag's Pyramid, the Seven-Point Structure, or the Three-Act Plot—you do not need to read every plot option. You can move directly to the steps that match your chosen framework.

For example:

If you plan to use **The Hero's Journey**, go directly to **Step 1B**, **Step 2B**, and the related sections.

If you prefer **Save the Cat**, jump to the Save the Cat steps.

If you selected **Freytag's Pyramid** or **Seven-Point Structure**, begin with the steps for those approaches.

Use the **Table of Contents** to quickly find the plot structure you want and follow only the steps connected to that specific framework. You can return to the other structures at any time for comparison, reference, or inspiration.

Step 1: Understanding Plot Structures

The plot is the foundation of your novel. It guides your story from the opening moment to the final scene and gives the reader a sense of direction and purpose. Before you begin shaping chapters and scenes, it helps you to choose a plot structure that matches the type of story you want to tell. There are many systems available, but five are especially well known and widely used. These structures appear in books, films, and play across genres because they offer reliable frameworks that support a strong narrative arc.

The Three Act Structure

The Three Act Structure divides a story into three main sections. Act One introduces the protagonist, their world, and the central problem. Act Two places the character under pressure and increases the complications standing in the way. Act Three brings everything to a peak and ends with the final resolution. This structure is familiar to readers because it creates a steady rhythm of setup, escalation, and payoff.

Example: Pride and Prejudice
Act One introduces Elizabeth Bennet's world and the social pressures surrounding her family.
Act Two builds tension through misunderstandings and shifting relationships, especially with Darcy.
Act Three resolves the central conflict as truths come to light and final relationships settle into place.

Example: Dracula
Act One establishes Jonathan Harker's journey to Transylvania.
Act Two heightens danger as Dracula travels to England and the conflict spreads.
Act Three concludes with the pursuit and final confrontation in Transylvania.

When Not to Use This Structure
Avoid this structure when your story moves across multiple timelines or relies on unconventional narrative order. Because the Three Act Structure

builds toward a single central climax, it does not support stories that depend on several equal peaks or layered revelations scattered throughout the plot. It is also not ideal for novels that focus more on atmosphere, theme, or internal reflection than on external conflict. If your narrative does not follow a clear progression of rising tension, you may find yourself forcing the story into a shape that does not fit its natural rhythm.

The Hero's Journey

The Hero's Journey focuses on transformation. The character begins in an ordinary world, receives a call to adventure, crosses into a new environment, faces trials, gains insight or power, and returns changed. This structure is useful when the heart of the story is about growth, discovery, identity, or self-realization.

Example: The Odyssey
Odysseus begins in the ordinary world of Ithaca.
The call to adventure occurs when he leaves for the Trojan War.
Trials follow as he faces monsters, temptations, and obstacles on his return journey.
He returns home changed and wiser.

Example: Alice's Adventures in Wonderland
Alice begins in her ordinary world.
The call to adventure arrives when she follows the White Rabbit.
Trials occur as she encounters strange creatures and challenges.
She returns from Wonderland with new understanding.

When Not to Use This Structure
Avoid this structure when your story does not focus on a clear internal transformation. The Hero's Journey depends on a deep shift in identity, belief, or emotional state. If your protagonist is meant to remain stable or simply solve an external problem without personal change, this structure will feel forced. It also works poorly for ensemble casts because the journey centers on a single hero. If your story does not include a return to an "ordinary world," or if your character never fully commits to a quest, the movement through its stages may not match your intentions.

Save the Cat Beat Sheet

Save the Cat uses fifteen beats that track emotional movement and story progression. These beats create natural pacing and help maintain a satisfying flow. Key moments include the opening image, the catalyst, the midpoint shift, and the finale. Writers often use this structure because it combines plot movement with character development in a clear sequence.

Example: A Christmas Carol
The opening image shows Scrooge's cold routine.
The catalyst arrives with Marley's ghost.
The midpoint occurs when Scrooge sees what awaits him if he does not change.
The finale shows his transformation into a generous man.

Example: The Secret Garden
The opening shows Mary Lennox isolated and unhappy.
The catalyst appears when she discovers the locked garden.
The midpoint brings renewed life as the garden begins to flourish.
The finale shows Mary and Colin transformed by healing.

When Not to Use This Structure
Avoid this structure when you prefer a loose or exploratory writing style that evolves without predetermined turning points. Save the Cat is highly structured and depends on specific emotional beats occurring in a particular order. If you do not want to shape your story around fixed moments such as the catalyst or the midpoint, it may feel restrictive. It also does not work well for stories that rely on ambiguous pacing or subtle shifts rather than strong, clearly defined moments of change.

Freytag's Pyramid

Freytag's Pyramid is based on dramatic tension and release. It includes exposition, rising action, climax, falling action, and resolution. It is shaped like a peak, with the climax at the highest point. This structure works well for tragedies, dramas, and stories with strong emotional arcs or moral consequences.

   Example: Hamlet
Exposition introduces Hamlet and the court of Denmark.
Rising action builds as Hamlet seeks the truth about his father's death.
The climax occurs during the confrontation that exposes betrayal and violence.
Falling action follows as the court unravels.
The resolution concludes with the deaths of the major characters and the restoration of order.

   Example: Frankenstein
Exposition presents Victor Frankenstein and his early ambitions.
Rising action follows the creation of the creature and the consequences that unfold.
The climax comes as the creature confronts Victor with devastating demands.
Falling action tracks their pursuit across difficult terrain.
The resolution ends with the deaths of both creator and creation.

   When Not to Use This Structure
Avoid this structure when your story contains several smaller climaxes rather than one major peak. Freytag's Pyramid depends on a single high point of tension, which does not suit stories built around episodic quests, mystery clues, or a chain of interconnected plotlines. It also struggles with ensemble stories where multiple character arcs peak at different times. If your narrative thrives on twists, reversals, or surprises scattered throughout, this model may restrict the natural movement of your story.

The Seven Point Plot Structure

The Seven Point Plot Structure uses seven major turning points that mark key movements of the story. These include the hook, the first plot point, pinch points that increase pressure, the midpoint where the character's direction changes, a second plot point that prepares the final act, and the concluding resolution. It is popular among fantasy and science fiction writers because it offers focus without requiring a long list of beats.

Example: Treasure Island

The hook shows Jim Hawkins at the inn.
The first plot point occurs when he discovers the map.
Pinch points appear through early dangers from pirates.
The midpoint shifts once the island is reached and alliances change.
The second plot point prepares the final confrontation with the mutineers.
The resolution brings the return home with the treasure secured.

Example: Jane Eyre

The hook introduces Jane's difficult childhood.
The first plot point begins when she arrives at Thornfield.
Pinch points arise through strange events and rising tension.
The midpoint shifts when Jane learns unsettling truths.
The second plot point forces her to leave Thornfield.
The resolution brings her return, reconciliation, and stability.

When Not to Use This Structure

Avoid this structure when your story is driven more by internal exploration than external turning points. The Seven Point Structure depends on clearly defined shifts that guide the reader through a specific sequence of events. If your narrative moves through subtle emotional change rather than plot-driven moments, these points may feel artificial. It also may not suit discovery writers who prefer to uncover their story while drafting rather than mapping out the major beats beforehand. If your story grows organically through character choices rather than predetermined milestones, this framework may restrict your process.

Step 1A: The Three Act Structure – A Deeper Understanding

The Three Act Structure is one of the oldest and most widely used storytelling models. It organizes a story into three movements that guide the reader through setup, escalation, and resolution. Each act has a clear purpose and creates a rhythm that feels natural to most readers.

Act I: Setup

The first act establishes the world of the story. The goal is to create a stable foundation before conflict arrives. Readers meet the protagonist, understand their routines, see what they value, and sense their internal or external challenges. This act also introduces the central problem through the inciting incident. The moment this disruption occurs, the protagonist can no longer remain in the comfort of their old world. By the end of this act, the direction of the story becomes clear, and movement toward the central conflict begins.

Main purpose:
Prepare the reader for the journey. Introduce character, setting, tone, and the first sign of conflict. The protagonist's world changes in a way that forces action.

Act II: Confrontation

The second act is the heart of the story. Here the protagonist faces rising challenges and pressure that test their abilities and deepen the central conflict. Obstacles grow more complicated, relationships shift, and stakes become clearer. This act often includes a midpoint shift, where the protagonist learns something important or experiences an event that changes their approach. Tension builds steadily as the protagonist struggles, adapts, or fails. By the end of this act, the character is pushed to a breaking point that leads directly into the climax.

Main purpose:
Challenge the protagonist and raise the stakes. Reveal weaknesses and force

growth. Establish turning points that lead toward transformation and the final conflict.

Act III: Resolution

The final act brings the story to its highest moment of tension and then resolves the conflict. The protagonist faces the main obstacle head-on during the climax, using everything learned throughout the story. After this decisive moment, the narrative moves into the aftermath, where loose ends are tied up, emotional threads come to rest, and a new normal is established. The resolution shows the reader how the journey has changed the protagonist or their world.

Main purpose:
Deliver the payoff. Resolve the conflict, show transformation, and complete the story in a satisfying way.

Step 1B: The Hero's Journey – A Deeper Understanding

The Hero's Journey is a classic structure rooted in mythic storytelling. It follows a pattern of departure, transformation, and return. This structure works well when the heart of your story is about a character undergoing meaningful change. It is divided into stages, each with a purpose that supports the hero's growth.

The Ordinary World

Every Hero's Journey begins with a familiar environment. This opening stage shows the protagonist's daily life, relationships, routines, and limitations. It establishes what the hero considers normal and often hints at something missing. This grounding allows readers to see the contrast once the adventure begins.

Purpose:
Show the hero's starting point and what may need to change. Establish comfort, routine, or dissatisfaction.

The Call to Adventure

A problem, message, discovery, or event disrupts the ordinary world. The hero is invited or pushed toward a new path. This moment reveals the story's core conflict and signals that the status quo cannot hold.

Purpose:
Introduce the challenge that will reshape the hero's life. Show the moment when the story truly begins to move.

Refusal of the Call

The hero hesitates, denies, or avoids the call. Fear, duty, disbelief, or comfort keeps them from accepting the journey. This resistance highlights their vulnerability and reminds readers that change is never easy.

Purpose:
Show the hero's reluctance and the stakes of staying the same. Emphasize their humanity and internal conflict.

Meeting the Mentor

A guide, teacher, or ally appears to provide insight, wisdom, or encouragement. The mentor prepares the hero for the challenges ahead and helps them take the first step toward transformation.

Purpose:
Offer support that helps the hero commit to the journey. Clarify the path forward and strengthen the hero's resolve.

Crossing the Threshold

The hero leaves the ordinary world and steps into a new environment. This is a point of no return. The rules change, the stakes rise, and the hero faces challenges they have never encountered before.

Purpose:
Show the hero's commitment. Mark the shift from preparation to action.

Tests, Allies, and Enemies

The hero faces early challenges that test their abilities. They meet allies who offer support and enemies who oppose them. Through these interactions, the hero learns more about themselves, the world, and the true nature of the conflict.

Purpose:
Develop relationships, expand the world, and test the hero's strengths and flaws.

Approach to the Inmost Cave

The hero prepares for a major challenge, often the most dangerous part of the journey so far. Plans are made, doubts resurface, and tension rises. The hero must confront fear and uncertainty.

Purpose:
Build suspense and deepen the emotional stakes. Show the hero gathering strength for the ordeal ahead.

The Ordeal

This is the central crisis. The hero faces the core threat or undergoes a symbolic death. Everything is on the line. The ordeal marks the moment of highest risk so far and often transforms the hero in some significant way.

Purpose:
Push the hero to their limit. Reveal the cost of failure and open the door to true change.

Reward

After surviving the ordeal, the hero gains something valuable. This reward may be knowledge, power, understanding, or a literal object. It changes the hero's perspective and often provides what they need for the final part of the story.

Purpose:
Show growth, reflection, and renewed purpose. Provide the turning point that prepares the hero for the final conflict.

The Road Back

The hero begins the return to the ordinary world, but with new danger or consequences emerging. The enemy may strike back, or the world may react to the hero's victory. Tension builds toward the final confrontation.

Purpose:
Transition from triumph to a new threat. Set the stage for the climax.

The Resurrection

This is the final and most important challenge. The hero faces the ultimate test, often confronting a deeper internal conflict or making a defining choice. Transformation becomes complete through sacrifice, courage, insight, or acceptance.

Purpose:
Deliver the emotional and narrative peak. Show the hero proving their growth.

Return with the Elixir

The hero returns to the ordinary world, but changed. They bring back insight, healing, or a gift that benefits themselves or others. The world responds to their transformation, and a new normal begins.

Purpose:
Show the impact of the hero's journey. Demonstrate what has changed and why it matters.

Step 1C: Save the Cat Beat Sheet – A Deeper Understanding

Save the Cat is a plot structure built around fifteen beats that guide the emotional and narrative movement of a story. Each beat has a specific purpose and appears in a particular order. The structure works because it balances plot progression with character growth, giving the reader a steady rhythm of setup, tension, transformation, and resolution. Below is an overview of the fifteen beats and the main point of each one.

Opening Image

The story begins with a snapshot of the protagonist's current life. This moment reveals their emotional state, habits, flaws, and worldview. It sets the tone and shows what needs to change.

Purpose:
Introduce the starting point so readers can later see the contrast after transformation.

Theme Stated

Another character briefly hints at the story's lesson or emotional takeaway. The protagonist usually rejects or dismisses it, which underscores their current limitations.

Purpose:
Reflect the deeper message the protagonist will eventually learn.

Set Up

This beat expands the opening by showing the protagonist's relationships, responsibilities, and struggles. It presents what the protagonist cares about and what they might lose if they do not change.

Purpose:
Establish the emotional stakes and prepare the reader for the coming disruption.

Catalyst

A major event or discovery disrupts the protagonist's world. It breaks their routine and forces them to confront a situation they cannot ignore.

Purpose:
Launch the story's central conflict and signal that the old life is no longer sustainable.

Debate

The protagonist hesitates. They consider the risks, question their ability, or cling to old habits. This beat shows internal conflict and fear.

Purpose:
Give the protagonist space to resist change before fully committing to the journey.

Break into Two

The protagonist makes a decisive choice or is pushed into a new situation. They leave the comfort of Act One and enter a new world with different rules and challenges.

Purpose:
Mark the transition from reaction to action.

B Story

Another character enters who provides emotional support or thematic contrast. This person helps the protagonist grow or understand the deeper lesson of the story.

Purpose:
Add balance, connection, and thematic reinforcement.

Fun and Games

This section shows the protagonist exploring the new world. It offers early successes, surprises, or moments of excitement. The tone is often lighter here.

Purpose:
Highlight the promise of the new journey and show the contrast from Act One.

Midpoint

A major event changes everything. It can be a victory that feels like a loss or a setback that reveals new truth. The stakes rise sharply, and the story accelerates.

Purpose:
Shift the direction of the story and force the protagonist to become more active.

Bad Guys Close In

Internal and external pressures increase. Problems grow more complicated, and the protagonist struggles to maintain control. Doubts reappear, and relationships may strain.

Purpose:
Tighten tension and push the protagonist toward crisis.

All Is Lost

A devastating setback hits the protagonist. Something vital is lost, and they reach their lowest emotional point. This beat often mirrors the opening image but in a darker form.

Purpose:
Strip the protagonist of old beliefs or support systems so change becomes necessary.

Dark Night of the Soul

The protagonist grieves, reflects, or confronts their inner truth. It is a quiet moment where they process the pain of the previous beat and gain clarity.

Purpose:
Prepare the protagonist for transformation by forcing introspection.

Break into Three

A new decision or realization pushes the protagonist into the final act. They accept the story's theme and believe in a new approach or identity.

Purpose:
Mark the moment where the protagonist chooses growth.

Finale

The protagonist applies everything they have learned. They confront the central problem, solve it through growth, and integrate their new understanding. The story's conflicts resolve in a clear sequence of action and emotional validation.

Purpose:
Demonstrate the protagonist's evolution and resolve the external conflict.

Final Image

The closing moment reflects the change from the opening image. It shows the protagonist's new life or mindset, creating symmetry and closure.

Purpose:
Show lasting transformation and leave the reader with a clear emotional impression.

Step 1D: Freytag's Pyramid – A Deeper Understanding

Freytag's Pyramid is a classical structure built on the rise and fall of dramatic tension. It follows a five-part movement that resembles the shape of a peak. This model is especially effective for stories with a strong emotional arc, clear moral direction, or a focus on cause and consequence. Each stage contributes to the gradual build toward a single defining climax and a measured descent toward resolution.

Exposition

The exposition establishes the story's foundation. It presents the setting, introduces the protagonist, and clarifies the social or emotional environment. Readers learn what feels normal and what the protagonist values. Early hints of tension or imbalance often appear here to foreshadow coming conflict.

Purpose:
Ground the reader and prepare them for the shift from stability to disruption.

Rising Action

The rising action forms the largest portion of Freytag's structure. Here the conflict grows through a series of complications, challenges, or escalating pressures. New characters enter, relationships develop, and opposing forces gain strength. Each event raises the stakes and narrows the protagonist's options. This part of the story builds steadily toward the climax.

Purpose:
Increase tension through layered conflict and deepen the story's emotional and narrative complexity.

Climax

The climax is the turning point at the peak of the pyramid. It is the moment of greatest tension where the protagonist faces the central conflict directly. Decisions made here have irreversible consequences. This stage often determines the emotional direction of the falling action that follows.

Purpose:
Deliver the story's most intense moment and define the final trajectory of the narrative.

Falling Action

After the climax, the story shifts into falling action. The consequences of the protagonist's choices unfold. Relationships, conflicts, and loose ends begin to resolve. Tension gradually decreases as the narrative moves toward closure, but the emotional impact of the climax continues to shape events.

Purpose:
Show the aftermath of the peak moment and guide the reader toward final resolution.

Denouement

The denouement completes the story. It restores stability, clarifies remaining questions, and shows what the world or protagonist looks like after the events of the story. This stage often emphasizes reflection, healing, or a return to order.

Purpose:
Provide closure and show how the story's events have changed the protagonist or their world.

Step 1E: The Seven Point Plot Structure – A Deeper Understanding

The Seven Point Plot Structure is built around seven major turning points that guide the story from the initial situation to the final resolution. This structure focuses on the most important shifts in direction, pressure, and character development. It is especially useful for writers who want a clear framework without relying on long lists of beats. Each point represents a defined change in the character's journey.

The Hook

The hook shows the protagonist in their starting state. It introduces who they are before the main conflict begins. This moment often highlights a flaw, a lack, or an imbalance that hints at what the character must eventually confront or grow beyond.

Purpose:
Show the reader the baseline of the protagonist's life and establish what needs to change.

First Plot Point

The first plot point pushes the protagonist out of their ordinary world and into the main conflict. It is often a disruptive event or a decision that shifts the story's direction. The protagonist enters a new situation they cannot easily escape.

Purpose:
Launch the main story by moving the protagonist from stability into challenge.

First Pinch Point

The first pinch point applies pressure and reveals the strength of the opposing force. It shows the reader what is at risk and reminds the protagonist that the conflict is real and dangerous.

Purpose:
Raise tension and increase awareness of the stakes through external pressure.

Midpoint

The midpoint marks a major shift in understanding, purpose, or strategy. It is the moment where the protagonist becomes more active and begins taking control of their journey. The conflict deepens, and the stakes become more personal or urgent.

Purpose:
Transform the protagonist's approach and move the story into a new and more intense phase.

Second Pinch Point

The second pinch point pushes the protagonist harder and reveals the consequences of failure more clearly. This point often exposes a weakness, creates significant loss, or tightens the antagonist's grip on the situation.

Purpose:
Increase tension through meaningful setbacks and sharpen the story's direction toward the final act.

Second Plot Point

The second plot point introduces the final piece of information, insight, or motivation the protagonist needs to face the climax. It may be a revelation, a discovery, a recovered resource, or a strengthened emotional resolve.

Purpose:
Prepare the protagonist for the final confrontation by giving them what they lacked before.

Resolution

The resolution delivers the conclusion of the story. The protagonist confronts the central conflict, applies what they have learned, and resolves the primary tension. The ending shows how the protagonist has changed and how the story's events have reshaped their world.

Purpose:
Provide closure and demonstrate the impact of the character's journey and choices.

Activity Step 1: Choosing Your Plot Structure

Now that you have explored the five major plot structures, take time to select the one that feels right for the story you want to create. There is no correct or incorrect choice. Pick the model that matches the type of journey you want your characters to take and the way you naturally think about storytelling.

Begin by choosing one of the following:

The Three Act Structure
The Hero's Journey
Save the Cat Beat Sheet
Freytag's Pyramid
The Seven Point Plot Structure

Once you have made your choice, open a journal, notebook, notepad, or word processor. You may use any writing method that feels comfortable, whether it is handwritten pages or digital notes. At the top of the page, write the name of your chosen plot structure. Underneath, list the main plot points or stages that belong to that structure. Do not worry about filling in details yet. Simply write out the major steps so you can see the full shape of your story's foundation.

Your task is to copy the structure in its simplest form, using the divisions you studied in Step 1. For example, if you choose the Hero's Journey, write out the stages such as the Ordinary World, Call to Adventure, Refusal, and so on. If you choose Save the Cat, write out the fifteen beats in order. If you choose the Three Act Structure, list Act One, Act Two, and Act Three with their key turning moments. Use the style that matches your chosen structure.

The goal of this activity is to help you understand the overall movement of your story before you begin planning chapters or scenes. Seeing the major steps laid out clearly will make the next stages of this workbook much easier. Take your time and write out each point with space beneath it, since you will return to these notes later as your story grows.

Step 2: Understanding Chapters

Chapters are the larger sections that shape the flow of your novel. They help the reader move through the story in clear, manageable steps, and they give the writer a simple way to organize ideas, events, and emotional changes. While plots give your story direction, chapters give it structure. They break the journey into readable portions that feel natural and easy to follow.

Every chapter serves a purpose. Some chapters introduce new problems. Others deepen the tension, shift relationships, or reveal information the reader needs to understand what comes next. Chapters can be short or long, calm or intense, but they should always move the story forward in some meaningful way. A chapter does not exist just to fill space. It exists to show progress.

A chapter's internal structure can vary depending on what your story needs. Some chapters contain one important scene. Others include several scenes that build on each other to create a meaningful change. What matters is that each chapter begins with a clear intention, unfolds through focused scenes, and ends with a sense of movement, whether that movement is emotional, narrative, or both.

In this step, you will learn how chapters work, how they support your plot, and how to begin shaping chapters that fit your story. Step 2A through Step 2E will guide you through the purpose of chapters, how to plan them, how to pace them, and how to use them to build a strong and engaging story.

Before moving forward, remind yourself that chapters do not have to be perfect in the planning stage. You are simply learning how to structure them clearly so your later writing becomes easier and more confident.

Step 2A: Chapters in the Three Act Structure

Chapters in the Three Act Structure follow a pattern of rising involvement. Each chapter contributes a small but meaningful step toward the overall movement of setup, confrontation, and resolution. While the exact number of chapters varies from novel to novel, the purpose of each chapter within its act remains consistent. The Complete Guideline for the Three Act Structure breaks these acts into chapters with clear functions, and understanding those functions will help you shape your own chapter plan later in this workbook.

Chapters in Act I: Setup

Act I chapters introduce the world of your novel and set the foundation readers need before the central conflict unfolds. Early chapters focus on establishing the setting, atmosphere, tone, and the protagonist's daily life. These chapters often contain quieter moments that show the reader what "normal" looks like for the character.

As Act I progresses, chapters begin to reveal subtle disruptions. These interruptions might be emotional unease, a minor conflict, or small hints of trouble. By the time you reach the later chapters of Act I, the story is building toward the inciting incident. The last chapter of this act usually contains the event that breaks the protagonist's routine and forces them to move toward change.

Example from the guideline style:
In the guideline, Chapter One is dedicated to introducing the world and the protagonist. Subsequent chapters show routine, small disruptions, and rising pressure, until Chapter Four delivers the inciting incident and the first strong reaction to it.

Public-domain illustration:
In Pride and Prejudice, the early chapters establish the Bennet family, social expectations, and Elizabeth's perspective. Each chapter adds detail to her world while quietly pointing toward future conflict, such as Mr. Bingley's arrival and Darcy's first slight. These chapters lay the groundwork for the shifts that will soon disrupt Elizabeth's assumptions.

Purpose of Act I chapters:
Introduce the world, clarify what the protagonist values, and show why the coming conflict will matter. Every chapter gently guides the reader toward the moment where the story truly begins.

Chapters in Act II: Confrontation

Act II contains the majority of the novel's chapters, and this is where complexity deepens. Chapters in this act introduce obstacles, new characters, shifting alliances, and the consequences of the protagonist's early choices. Each chapter should create a sense of movement, whether through plot events, character decisions, or emotional development.

In the guideline, Act II chapters often begin with the protagonist entering unfamiliar territory, then steadily layering failure, tension, and growth. These chapters also include pivotal moments such as the midpoint, where a revelation or major event shifts the story in a new direction. Later chapters in Act II press harder on the protagonist, narrowing their options and bringing them to crisis.

Example from the guideline style:
Chapters Five through Fourteen handle increasing challenges, new alliances, rising threats, the midpoint shift, and the lead-up to the "all is lost" moment. Each chapter refines the protagonist's arc and tightens the conflict.

Public-domain illustration:
In Dracula, the early chapters of Act II follow Harker's escape attempt and the introduction of Mina, Lucy, and Van Helsing. Later chapters intensify the conflict as Lucy deteriorates and Dracula's influence grows. Each chapter heightens the danger and narrows the characters' choices, pushing them toward the story's central crisis.

Purpose of Act II chapters:
Increase pressure, complicate the protagonist's path, and reveal the deeper layers of conflict. Each chapter forces the protagonist to adjust, struggle, fail, or grow as the story moves toward its breaking point.

Chapters in Act III: Resolution

Act III chapters turn the tension of Act II into decisive action. Early chapters in this act often show the protagonist preparing for the final confrontation. These chapters stabilize the story after the crisis and focus the protagonist's resolve. The central climax appears near the end of the act, where the protagonist uses everything they have learned to face the main conflict.

The final chapters resolve subplots, restore order, and show how the protagonist has changed. These chapters do not need to be long or complex, but they must provide clear closure for the reader.

Example from the guideline style:
Chapters Fifteen through Eighteen include preparation for the final conflict, the confrontation itself, the aftermath, and the return to stability. The final chapter shows the protagonist's new normal.

Public-domain illustration:
In Pride and Prejudice, the final chapters resolve misunderstandings, reveal Darcy's true character, and conclude with Elizabeth's acceptance of his proposal. Each chapter in this act ties emotional threads together and brings the story to a satisfying end.

Purpose of Act III chapters:
Deliver resolution, show transformation, and complete the story with clarity. Each chapter answers remaining questions and reestablishes balance after the climax.

Step 2B: Chapters in the Hero's Journey

Chapters in the Hero's Journey follow the rhythm of transformation. While the number of chapters depends on the length and style of the novel, each chapter in this structure serves a specific purpose within the broader arc of departure, initiation, and return. The Complete Guideline shows how each stage of the journey is represented through one or more chapters. Your goal is to understand what chapters must accomplish at each stage before you begin planning your own.

Chapters in the Ordinary World

Chapters in this stage introduce the protagonist's life before the adventure begins. These chapters show familiar routines, relationships, values, flaws, and sources of dissatisfaction. The tone is stable, but there are small signs that something in the hero's life feels incomplete. These chapters help readers understand the starting point the hero will eventually grow beyond.

Example from the guideline style:
Chapter One shows the hero's daily life and introduces traits that will be tested during the journey.

Public-domain illustration:
In Alice's Adventures in Wonderland, the opening chapters show Alice's boredom and curiosity, setting the stage for the extraordinary world she is about to enter.

Purpose of these chapters:
Ground the reader in the hero's current life and reveal what needs to change.

Chapters in the Call to Adventure

Chapters here introduce the problem, message, or event that disrupts the hero's ordinary world. These chapters demonstrate that the hero cannot continue as they are. The call may be exciting, frightening, mysterious, or disruptive, but it always pushes the story forward.

Example from the guideline style:
A chapter presents a message or discovery that reveals the coming conflict, followed by the hero's immediate reaction in the next chapter.

Public-domain illustration:
In The Odyssey, the call to adventure is set long before Odysseus's return journey, but the chapters describing the news of the Trojan War and the obligation to fight serve as the initial call toward a long arc of trials.

Purpose of these chapters:
Introduce the central conflict and push the hero toward change.

Chapters in the Refusal of the Call

These chapters show the hero's hesitation or resistance. The reasons may be emotional, practical, or rooted in fear. The hero may try to maintain normalcy, ignore the call, or rationalize their reluctance. The tension builds as consequences of inaction begin to emerge.

Example from the guideline style:
One chapter displays the hero's avoidance, and the next shows pressure increasing through consequences or worsening circumstances.

Public-domain illustration:
In The Hobbit (not public-domain yet; avoid)
Better alternative: In many Arthurian legends, including older public-domain versions, young Arthur initially resists the responsibilities placed on him, showing reluctance to accept his destiny before taking up the sword.

Purpose of these chapters:
Show the emotional weight of the journey and heighten the significance of accepting the call.

Chapters in Meeting the Mentor

These chapters introduce a mentor who provides wisdom, guidance, or encouragement. The mentor helps the hero understand the path ahead and prepares them for the unknown. Chapters in this stage often reveal important tools, knowledge, or insight.

Example from the guideline style:
One chapter shows the initial meeting, and another focuses on the mentor's teaching or influence.

Public-domain illustration:
In The Odyssey, Athena frequently appears in chapters that guide Odysseus or his son Telemachus, offering support and wisdom that prepare them for difficult challenges.

Purpose of these chapters:
Give the hero the clarity or courage they need to step into the adventure.

Chapters in Crossing the Threshold

These chapters mark the hero's transition from the ordinary world into the unfamiliar one. The threshold crossing might involve physical travel, an emotional commitment, or a symbolic choice. These chapters typically show the hero taking a step they cannot reverse.

Example from the guideline style:
One chapter shows the decision to go, followed by a chapter that marks the first steps into the new world.

Public-domain illustration:
In Alice's Adventures in Wonderland, the chapter where Alice falls down the rabbit hole marks her threshold crossing into the strange and unpredictable world of Wonderland.

Purpose of these chapters:
Shift the story from preparation to engagement with the central conflict.

Chapters in Tests, Allies, and Enemies

These chapters make up a significant portion of the Hero's Journey. The hero encounters new allies who offer help, enemies who create obstacles, and challenges that test their abilities. Each chapter should reveal new aspects of the world and the hero's character. Failures and small successes both shape the hero's growth.

Example from the guideline style:
Chapters show a first test, a recovery from failure, the introduction of allies, cooperation among characters, and early confrontations with enemies.

Public-domain illustration:
In The Odyssey, much of the middle portion follows this pattern: encounters with the Cyclops, Circe, and the Sirens test Odysseus's skill and resolve while shaping his understanding of himself and the world.

Purpose of these chapters:
Develop the hero's skills, build relationships, and increase tension as the journey grows more complicated.

Chapters in the Approach to the Inmost Cave

These chapters focus on preparation for a major challenge. The hero plans, gathers resources, or reflects on fears. Complications may arise that test the hero's readiness. Tension rises as the story moves toward a significant turning point.

Example from the guideline style:
One chapter shows the group planning, and another shows the plan being disrupted or complicated.

Public-domain illustration:
In classical myth, Theseus preparing to enter the labyrinth serves as the approach stage before confronting the Minotaur.

Purpose of these chapters:
Build suspense and position the hero for the central crisis.

Chapters in the Ordeal

These chapters contain the central crisis of the story. The hero faces a major threat or challenge that forces them to confront their deepest fear or limitation. The ordeal often represents a symbolic or literal death and rebirth, creating permanent change.

Example from the guideline style:
One chapter focuses on entering the dangerous situation, and another shows the peak of the crisis and its immediate consequences.

Public-domain illustration:
In The Odyssey, the journey to the underworld serves as one of Odysseus's greatest ordeals, confronting death, fate, and prophecy.

Purpose of these chapters:
Push the hero to the breaking point to catalyze transformation.

Chapters in the Reward

These chapters show what the hero gains from surviving the ordeal. This reward may be knowledge, insight, an object of importance, or a new sense of identity. The reward prepares the hero for the final part of the journey.

Example from the guideline style:
A chapter shows recovery, and another focuses on the hero understanding the significance of what they gained.

Public-domain illustration:
Odysseus receiving advice and prophecy from the dead during his underworld journey becomes his reward: knowledge that guides the final stages of his return.

Purpose of these chapters:
Demonstrate how the ordeal has changed the hero and provide the tools needed for the final challenge.

Chapters in the Road Back

These chapters show the consequences of the ordeal and the urgency that follows. The enemy may retaliate, or new dangers may appear. The hero returns to the world of the conflict with renewed purpose.

Example from the guideline style:
One chapter shows the world reacting to the ordeal, and another shows the hero moving toward the final confrontation.

Public-domain illustration:
In many myths, the hero's return journey brings new challenges as forces attempt to stop them from completing their transformation.

Purpose of these chapters:
Transition from victory to new tension and lead the story into the final confrontation.

Chapters in the Resurrection

These chapters contain the true climax. The hero faces the ultimate test that represents the culmination of their journey. The final battle or decision reveals how much they have changed.

Example from the guideline style:
One chapter focuses on the final confrontation, followed by a chapter showing the hero's transformation.

Public-domain illustration:
In many Arthurian legends, Arthur's final battle against Mordred serves as the resurrection stage, where he confronts the consequences of his choices and identity.

Purpose of these chapters:
Demonstrate the hero's final transformation through decisive action.

Chapters in the Return with the Elixir

These chapters show the hero returning to the ordinary world, carrying the knowledge or gift gained from the journey. The world acknowledges the hero's transformation, and a new normal begins. Final chapters close remaining threads and reflect the story's lessons.

Example from the guideline style:
A chapter shows the hero's return, and a final chapter reveals how they share the elixir with the world.

Public-domain illustration:
In The Odyssey, the final chapters show Odysseus reclaiming his home, restoring order, and proving that his trials have changed him.

Purpose of these chapters:
Show the impact of the hero's transformation and restore stability.

Step 2C: Chapters in Save the Cat

Save the Cat is structured around fifteen beats, and although the beats are fixed, the chapters that support them can vary in placement and length. Chapters in a Save the Cat story exist to highlight emotional turning points and guide the protagonist through a clear series of shifts. The Complete Guideline focuses on scenes and beats, but its logic also reveals how chapters must function at the higher level. Each chapter supports one or more beats, and each beat marks a meaningful step in the story's progression.

Chapters Covering the Opening Image and Theme Stated

These early chapters introduce the protagonist's current life, showing both routine and dissatisfaction. They also present the story's theme through another character's comment or observation. Chapters in this stage are simple and focused: they show what must eventually change.

Example from the guideline style:
One chapter introduces the hero's world and mood, while the next chapter shows the stated theme through dialogue or observation.

Public-domain illustration:
In A Christmas Carol, early chapters focus on Scrooge's rigid habits and cold worldview, establishing what will need to shift later.

Purpose of these chapters:
Set the tone, reveal the starting point, and introduce the theme that will shape the protagonist's journey.

Chapters Supporting the Set Up

These chapters expand relationships, responsibilities, and pressures surrounding the protagonist. They prepare the reader for the coming disruption. Each chapter adds layers to the protagonist's emotional world, showing what they value and what they fear losing.

Example from the guideline style:
Chapters introduce the hero's connections and responsibilities while quietly raising tension.

Public-domain illustration:
In The Secret Garden, the early chapters build Mary Lennox's isolated world, showing her loneliness and lack of empathy before the catalyst appears.

Purpose of these chapters:
Build investment in the protagonist's life and clarify the emotional stakes.

Chapters Handling the Catalyst and Debate

These chapters present the event that shatters the protagonist's stability. The catalyst is followed by chapters where the protagonist hesitates, doubts themselves, or tries to avoid change. The debate section often spans multiple chapters, since characters rarely leap into transformation without resistance.

Example from the guideline style:
One chapter contains the catalyst event, followed by one or two chapters showing debate and internal conflict.

Public-domain illustration:
In A Christmas Carol, Marley's visit is the catalyst, and the following chapters show Scrooge grappling with fear and disbelief before agreeing to the journey.

Purpose of these chapters:
Introduce irreversible change and give the protagonist space to struggle with the decision to move forward.

Chapters Supporting Break into Two and B Story

Chapters in this stage shift the story into Act Two. The protagonist either chooses or is forced into a new situation. These chapters have a noticeable increase in energy. They also introduce an emotional or thematic support character who will help the protagonist grow.

Example from the guideline style:
A chapter shows the decision or forced transition, followed by a chapter introducing the B Story character.

Public-domain illustration:
In The Secret Garden, Mary's entry into the garden and her relationship with Dicken represent the shift into the new world and the strengthening presence of a supporting guide.

Purpose of these chapters:
Mark the beginning of the protagonist's active journey and establish the emotional support that will reinforce the theme.

Chapters Covering Fun and Games

Chapters in this section explore the promise of the premise. The protagonist experiments with the new world, encountering early challenges and successes. These chapters often carry a tone of curiosity or excitement, balanced by growing tension beneath the surface.

Example from the guideline style:
Chapters show the hero adjusting to the new environment and experiencing early victories or surprises.

Public-domain illustration:
In A Christmas Carol, Scrooge's early travels with the Ghost of Christmas Past show glimpses of joy and memory before deeper pain is revealed.

Purpose of these chapters:
Show the contrast between the old world and the new one, building engagement before tension rises.

Chapters Surrounding the Midpoint

The midpoint is a major turning point, often marked by a revelation, a false victory, or a stinging defeat. Chapters here shift the protagonist into more deliberate action. The tone becomes more urgent.

Example from the guideline style:
One chapter contains the midpoint event itself, followed by a chapter showing the protagonist reacting with new determination.

Public-domain illustration:
In A Christmas Carol, the midpoint occurs when Scrooge witnesses the present and sees the consequences of his behavior unfolding in real time, deepening his understanding.

Purpose of these chapters:
Transform the protagonist's mindset and change the story's direction.

Chapters Supporting Bad Guys Close In

These chapters intensify conflict. External antagonists push harder, and internal fears resurface. The protagonist struggles to keep control, and relationships may weaken. Each chapter increases pressure, narrowing the path to resolution.

Example from the guideline style:
Chapters show increased threats and emotional strain as the protagonist loses ground.

Public-domain illustration:
In The Secret Garden, setbacks and emotional challenges arise as characters confront fears and insecurities, tightening conflict before transformation.

Purpose of these chapters:
Build tension and accelerate movement toward the crisis.

Chapters Containing All Is Lost and Dark Night of the Soul

Here the protagonist experiences their lowest moment. These chapters often involve symbolic or literal loss. The Dark Night of the Soul chapter follows, giving the protagonist space to reflect on the failure and confront inner truths.

Example from the guideline style:
One chapter shows the devastating event, and the next shows the protagonist's reflection.

Public-domain illustration:
In A Christmas Carol, chapters depicting Scrooge's potential death and loneliness represent his "all is lost" moment, followed by introspection and grief.

Purpose of these chapters:
Break down the protagonist's old beliefs and prepare them for change.

Chapters Supporting Break into Three and the Finale

These chapters show the protagonist embracing a new understanding. A plan forms, allies regroup, and the protagonist steps into the final confrontation. The finale often spans multiple chapters, resolving external conflict first and emotional transformation second.

Example from the guideline style:
A chapter shows the fresh decision, followed by chapters where the plan is carried out and the core conflict is resolved.

Public-domain illustration:
In A Christmas Carol, the final chapters show Scrooge awakening changed and taking action that reflects his new identity.

Purpose of these chapters:
Complete the character's transformation and resolve the overall conflict.

Chapters that Provide the Final Image

The final chapter or chapters show the protagonist's new world. This image contrasts with the opening image to highlight what has changed.

Example from the guideline style:
One chapter shows the protagonist settling into their new normal.

Public-domain illustration:
A Christmas Carol ends with Scrooge becoming generous and warmhearted, clearly transformed from the opening chapters.

Purpose of these chapters:
Offer closure and demonstrate the long-term effects of the protagonist's growth.

Step 2D: Chapters in Freytag's Pyramid

Chapters in Freytag's Pyramid follow a clear rise and fall of dramatic tension. While the structure appears simple, each section requires focused chapters that gradually build or release pressure. Your Complete Guideline outlines how each movement is divided into chapters, and this step explains the purpose of those chapters at a conceptual level. This will help you shape your own chapters later in the workbook.

Chapters in the Exposition

Exposition chapters introduce the setting, characters, and social world. These chapters provide the stability the story needs before conflict begins. They often reveal relationships, establish tone, and hint at early disturbances. The goal is to help readers understand the protagonist's environment and what might be disrupted.

Example from the guideline style:
The early chapters show the ordinary world, key relationships, early tensions, and the first subtle sign that something is not right.

Public-domain illustration:
In Frankenstein, the opening chapters introduce Victor's family, upbringing, and intellectual fascinations. These chapters build the foundation for understanding why his ambitions lead to future consequences.

Purpose of these chapters:
Ground the reader and gently foreshadow the conflict that will drive the rising action.

Chapters in the Rising Action

These chapters make up a large portion of the story. Rising action chapters introduce problems, deepen conflict, and reveal new obstacles. Each chapter adds pressure and increases the complexity of the protagonist's situation. Relationships evolve, antagonists become clearer, and the story steadily builds toward a powerful climax.

Example from the guideline style:
Chapters show attempts to control the situation, mounting costs, allies and rivals emerging, turning points in strategy, mistakes, and escalating danger.

Public-domain illustration:
In Hamlet, the rising action includes the ghost's revelation, Hamlet's investigations, the play-within-a-play, rising suspicion, and the tightening atmosphere at court. Each chapter-like section increases tension and pushes the story toward its inevitable peak.

Purpose of these chapters:
Strengthen the narrative drive, expose vulnerabilities, and lead every thread toward a central crisis.

Chapters in the Climax

The climax chapters represent the highest point of tension. This is where the protagonist confronts the central conflict directly. These chapters are charged with emotional and narrative intensity. The outcome of the confrontation determines the direction of the falling action.

Example from the guideline style:
One chapter focuses on the confrontation itself, and the next reveals the decisive outcome.

Public-domain illustration:
In Macbeth, the climax occurs when Macbeth realizes that the prophecies have turned against him, culminating in his final battle. The intensity reaches its peak as the truth becomes unavoidable.

Purpose of these chapters:
Deliver the story's most powerful moment and set the stage for consequences that follow.

Chapters in the Falling Action

These chapters show the immediate aftermath of the climax. Conflicts begin to resolve, relationships adjust, and emotional responses unfold. The tension decreases, but important details still come to light. These chapters make sense of the climax and guide the reader toward closure.

Example from the guideline style:
Chapters show the world reacting to the climax, secondary conflicts resolving, and characters adjusting to the new reality.

Public-domain illustration:
In Hamlet, the falling action includes the unraveling of court relationships and the final revelations that clarify the tragic trajectory of the story.

Purpose of these chapters:
Untangle narrative threads and transition the reader toward resolution.

Chapters in the Denouement

The final chapters establish order after the upheaval. They show what the world looks like once the conflict has ended. These chapters often emphasize reflection, emotional settlement, renewed stability, or moral takeaway. They bring the story to a complete and satisfying close.

Example from the guideline style:
A final chapter shows the new normal, the protagonist's change, and the last emotional or symbolic note.

Public-domain illustration:
In Frankenstein, the denouement occurs in the final chapters on the ice, where Victor recounts his story and the creature appears one last time before disappearing into the distance.

Purpose of these chapters:
Provide closure and show how the story's events transformed the protagonist or the world.

Step 2E: Chapters in the Seven Point Plot Structure

Chapters in the Seven Point Plot Structure revolve around seven major turning points. Because this structure focuses on a small number of essential moments, chapters must work efficiently. Each chapter either sets up a turning point, carries the character into it, or responds to the change it creates. Your Complete Guideline shows how the seven points shape the overall flow of chapters. This step explains the purpose of those chapters so you can later map your story onto this model.

Chapters Around the Hook

Chapters connected to the hook show the protagonist's initial state. These chapters reveal what is lacking, unbalanced, or uncertain in the protagonist's life. The hook is not simply an opening scene; it is the foundation upon which the later transformation will be measured. These chapters tend to be reflective, observational, or focused on the character's environment and identity.

Example from the guideline style:
A chapter introduces the ordinary world and the protagonist's flaw or vulnerability, followed by a shift that hints at future disruption.

Public-domain illustration:
In Jane Eyre, the early chapters at Gateshead clearly establish Jane's isolation, mistreatment, and inner strength. These chapters form the hook that makes her later choices meaningful.

Purpose of these chapters:
Show the starting point of the character's arc and set emotional expectations.

Chapters Leading to the First Plot Point

These chapters gradually transition from stability to disruption. They introduce the first major change that propels the protagonist into the main story. The first plot point often appears near the end of the early chapters, changing the protagonist's direction dramatically. Chapters here help the reader understand why this shift is significant.

Example from the guideline style:
A chapter presents an unavoidable event that forces the protagonist into a new situation.

Public-domain illustration:
In Treasure Island, chapters surrounding the discovery of the map shift Jim's life from predictable routine to sudden adventure. The decision to leave home solidifies this first major plot point.

Purpose of these chapters:
Move the story from introduction to action and pull the protagonist into the main conflict.

Chapters Supporting the First Pinch Point

These chapters highlight pressure from the antagonist or opposing force. They show the protagonist what they are up against and why the conflict matters. The first pinch point is a reminder of danger. Chapters here often involve tension, uncertainty, or the first taste of real conflict.

Example from the guideline style:
A chapter shows an early confrontation or problem caused by the antagonist.

Public-domain illustration:
In The Lion, the Witch and the Wardrobe (not fully public domain worldwide, avoid).
Better example: In Dracula, early chapters in England reveal disturbing events surrounding Lucy's decline, which act as an early pinch point that exposes the threat.

Purpose of these chapters:
Increase tension and underline the stakes of the journey.

Chapters Surrounding the Midpoint

The midpoint changes the direction of the story. Chapters at this stage reveal new information or shift the protagonist's approach. These chapters often increase the protagonist's agency, turning them from a passive participant into an active force in the story. The tone becomes more urgent and focused.

Example from the guideline style:
One chapter contains the revelation or major shift, and the next shows how the protagonist's understanding has changed.

Public-domain illustration:
In Treasure Island, the moment the characters realize the alliances on the island are not what they appear transforms the entire direction of the story and deepens the conflict.

Purpose of these chapters:
Refocus the protagonist's path and elevate the urgency of the story.

Chapters Supporting the Second Pinch Point

The second pinch point applies heavier pressure. Chapters here reveal higher stakes, greater danger, and stronger opposition. The protagonist begins to feel the cost of failure more intensely. These chapters often expose a weakness or create a painful setback.

Example from the guideline style:
A chapter shows the antagonist gaining ground or striking a painful blow.

Public-domain illustration:
In Jane Eyre, chapters dealing with the mysterious events at Thornfield serve as a second pinch point, revealing deeper threats and emotional risk for Jane.

Purpose of these chapters:
Tighten tension and emphasize the difficulty of the road ahead.

Chapters Leading to the Second Plot Point

These chapters introduce the final piece of information, strategy, or emotional strength the protagonist needs for the last act. The second plot point usually appears near the end of these chapters, offering clarity or a decisive change that prepares the protagonist for resolution.

Example from the guideline style:
A chapter reveals vital information, followed by a chapter where the protagonist prepares mentally or emotionally for the climax.

Public-domain illustration:
In Treasure Island, chapters revealing Silver's shifting alliances act as a second plot point that pushes Jim toward decisive action.

Purpose of these chapters:
Set up the protagonist for decisive action and the final confrontation.

Chapters in the Resolution

Chapters in this final stage conclude the story. They show the protagonist applying what they learned, confronting the main conflict, and resolving the story's central tension. These chapters also tie up loose ends and reflect on the character's growth.

Example from the guideline style:
One chapter shows the final confrontation, and the last chapter shows the new stability.

Public-domain illustration:
In Jane Eyre, the final chapters resolve Jane's emotional and moral conflicts and establish her new life, concluding the story with clarity.

Purpose of these chapters:
Bring the character's journey full circle and conclude the narrative with emotional and thematic closure.

Activity Step 2: Expanding Your Plot Points into Chapters

In Step 1, you chose a plot structure and wrote down its major plot points or stages. You will now continue working on the same page or document. Do not start a new outline. Instead, you will add chapters beneath the plot points you already wrote.

Open the journal, notebook, tablet, or word processor you used earlier. Look at the list of plot points from Step 1. Under each plot point, leave some space. You are going to begin shaping the chapters that will carry your story from one point to the next.

Beneath the first plot point, write a short note describing what the chapter or chapters in this section should accomplish. Use the explanations from Step 2 to guide you. For example, if your first plot point appears in the Three Act Structure, the chapters before it will introduce the protagonist's world and reveal early pressure. If you are using the Hero's Journey, the chapters beneath the Ordinary World will show the hero's daily life and their first signs of longing or imbalance. Continue this process for each plot point in your structure, adding chapter purposes underneath as needed.

You do not need to plan precise chapter counts or titles. You are only identifying what each chapter should do to support the major points of your plot. Add as many chapter purposes as you feel your story requires. Some plot points may need several chapters, while others may need only one. Follow the natural rhythm of your chosen structure.

When you finish, you should have your plot points from Step 1 followed by the beginnings of a chapter map that explains how your story will move from one moment to the next. Leave space under each chapter purpose. You will fill in the scenes during Step 3.

Step 3: Understanding Scenes

A scene is the smallest complete unit of storytelling in your novel. It unfolds in real time and shows the reader an event that changes something for the protagonist. Scenes carry the direct movement of your story forward. They are more focused than chapters and more active than beats. Each scene has a purpose, a goal, a conflict, and a shift that separates its ending from its beginning.

In Step 2, you added chapters beneath the plot points you chose in Step 1. Chapters are containers. Now we fill those containers with scenes. Every chapter should have one to three scenes, each contributing to the chapter's purpose and supporting the larger plot structure. By the end of Step 3, you will be able to take your chapters and expand them into clear scene ideas that move the story from moment to moment.

Scenes operate on three levels. They serve the plot structure by pushing the story toward the next major point. They support the chapter by fulfilling the chapter's purpose. They express character movement by showing what the protagonist wants in the moment, how they pursue it, and how they respond when something stands in their way.

A strong scene includes the following elements.

A clear purpose
The scene must justify its presence. It should reveal information, develop character, raise stakes, or move the story closer to conflict or resolution.

A character goal or desire
Someone in the scene wants something. The goal may be small, such as getting a piece of information, or large, such as escaping danger.

Conflict or resistance
Something blocks the goal. The obstacle may be external, such as an antagonist, or internal, such as doubt or fear.

A shift or outcome
By the end of the scene, something has changed. The protagonist succeeds, fails, is delayed, or learns something new.

Emotional or narrative movement

The character's emotional state should not be the same at the end as it was at the beginning. Even a subtle shift gives the scene meaning.

These elements form the foundation of your scenes. How they appear will depend on the plot structure you chose. Each structure distributes scenes differently across chapters, depending on how the story rises, turns, and resolves. In the following sections, you will learn how scenes function within each plot structure. You will also see examples drawn from public-domain literature to show how scenes support chapter purposes and plot movement.

Continue using your notes from Steps 1 and 2. You will add scenes directly beneath each chapter you already outlined. You are not writing the scenes in full, only identifying their purpose and movement. Leave space beneath each scene; you will fill in beats in Step 4.

Now let us explore how scenes work in each major plot structure.

Step 3A: Scenes in the Three Act Structure

Using the complete guideline structure, with Dracula examples only for illustration.

I will now start writing **Chapter One**, following your template:

Chapter purpose

Scene 1 (guideline-based) + Dracula example

Scene 2 (guideline-based) + Dracula example

...and so on through all 18 chapters.

Chapter One: Introduction to the World

Purpose of the Chapter

Introduce the setting and tone of the story. Present the protagonist and establish the atmosphere of the world before the main conflict disrupts it.

Scene 1: Establish the setting and tone

Guideline Purpose:
This scene grounds the reader. It shows where the story begins, what the world feels like, and the general mood of the opening. This may include sensory detail, daily routines, or early hints of unease.

Dracula Example:
Jonathan Harker enters a foreign village where the locals behave nervously, hinting at a world different from his own.

Scene 2: Initial character moment

Guideline Purpose:
This scene introduces the protagonist through action or reaction. A revealing trait, habit, or attitude appears here, helping the reader understand who they are before the story's changes begin.

Dracula Example:
Harker notes his curiosity and professionalism as he tries to interpret the locals' warnings, showing early traits that will matter later.

Chapter Two: Establish the Character's Normal Life

Purpose of the Chapter

Show the protagonist's daily routine and reveal what they value, how they behave, and how their ordinary world functions.

Scene 1: Show daily routine

Guideline Purpose:
This scene illustrates the character's normal patterns, relationships, and responsibilities. It highlights comfort zones and anchors the reader in the protagonist's everyday life.

Dracula Example:
Harker writes in his journal, documenting his travel notes and business responsibilities.

Scene 2: Light conflict appears

Guideline Purpose:
A small disruption interrupts the routine. This conflict foreshadows the larger trouble ahead and begins shifting the tone.

Dracula Example:
Harker notices that the carriage driver avoids sunlight and behaves strangely, unsettling him.

Chapter Three: Setting the Stakes

Purpose of the Chapter

Reveal what the protagonist has to gain or lose. Introduce early pressure that signals the importance of coming events.

Scene 1: Show what can be gained or lost

Guideline Purpose:
The scene clarifies the personal stakes for the protagonist. It shows what matters to them or what might be threatened in the future.

Dracula Example:
Harker realizes his assignment is important for his career, but the unsettling environment threatens his sense of stability.

Scene 2: Pressure increases

Guideline Purpose:
The scene escalates tension slightly, pushing the protagonist toward change. The situation becomes harder to ignore.

Dracula Example:
Harker sees Dracula behaving unnaturally, making it harder to dismiss earlier unease.

Chapter Four: The Inciting Incident

Purpose of the Chapter
Introduce the major disruptive event that alters the protagonist's path and forces engagement with the central conflict.

Scene 1: The major disruptive event

Guideline Purpose:
This scene breaks the protagonist's normal world. It presents a conflict that cannot be avoided or ignored.

Dracula Example:
The vampire brides attempt to bite Harker, revealing the true supernatural threat.

Scene 2: First reaction

Guideline Purpose:
The protagonist reacts emotionally or physically. They may try to deny or escape the situation, but the shift toward Act II begins.

Dracula Example:
Harker panics and recognizes he is trapped, beginning to consider escape.

Chapter Five: First Steps into the New World

Purpose of the Chapter
The protagonist enters a new situation where the rules change and early challenges begin to appear.

Scene 1: Entering unfamiliar territory
Guideline Purpose:
Show the protagonist stepping into a different environment. This may be a new physical location, a shift in relationship dynamics, or a change in expectations. The protagonist feels out of place.
Dracula Example:
Harker explores parts of the castle he has never seen before and begins noticing strange architectural impossibilities.

Scene 2: First conflict in the new world
Guideline Purpose:
Introduce a challenge the protagonist is not prepared for. The problem should hint at larger dangers to come.
Dracula Example:
Harker encounters a locked room that holds evidence of Dracula's predatory behavior.

Chapter Six: Early Attempts and First Failures

Purpose of the Chapter
The protagonist begins applying early strategies to handle the conflict but faces difficulty or failure.

Scene 1: First plan is attempted
Guideline Purpose:
Show the protagonist taking action based on what they understand so far. The plan should falter or fail.
Dracula Example:
Harker attempts to send letters secretly, but Dracula intercepts them.

Scene 2: Reveal of new obstacles
Guideline Purpose:
Show the introduction of a complication that wasn't previously visible. The antagonist's strength or influence becomes clearer.

Dracula Example:
Harker discovers that the castle has no servants and that Dracula performs tasks silently at night.

Chapter Seven: Building Alliances and Resources

Purpose of the Chapter
The protagonist begins gaining support or tools that will help them, even if imperfectly.

Scene 1: Allies appear
Guideline Purpose:
Introduce supportive characters or internal strengths. This may be emotional support, skills, or a symbolic resource.
Dracula Example:
Harker finds a few old books and maps that help him understand parts of the castle.

Scene 2: Plan formation
Guideline Purpose:
The protagonist and allies (if any) start forming a plan to address the conflict.
Dracula Example:
Harker maps a potential escape route after studying the castle layout.

Chapter Eight: Rising Challenges

Purpose of the Chapter
The conflict intensifies. The protagonist struggles to adapt while internal or external pressure builds.

Scene 1: Conflict intensifies
Guideline Purpose:
Introduce a stronger or more dangerous obstacle.
Dracula Example:

Harker witnesses Dracula's supernatural strength firsthand when he sees him carrying a heavy box with ease.

Scene 2: A deeper struggle
Guideline Purpose:
Reveal an internal flaw, fear, or misjudgment that worsens the situation.
Dracula Example:
Harker hesitates to escape due to fear of the unknown outside, highlighting his growing despair.

Chapter Nine: Midpoint Shift

Purpose of the Chapter
A major event transforms the protagonist's understanding of the conflict. Stakes escalate sharply.

Scene 1: Major event changes direction
Guideline Purpose:
Introduce a turning point that alters the story's trajectory.
Dracula Example:
Harker finds evidence that Dracula plans to travel to England, widening the threat beyond the castle.

Scene 2: Protagonist gains new clarity
Guideline Purpose:
Show the protagonist becoming more deliberate and active.
Dracula Example:
Harker realizes he must escape not only for himself but to prevent greater harm.

Chapter Ten: Turning Pressure Upward

Purpose of the Chapter
External forces increase tension and internal doubts return. The protagonist loses ground.

Scene 1: External forces apply pressure
Guideline Purpose:
Show the antagonist or situation becoming more pressing.
Dracula Example:
Dracula becomes more suspicious of Harker's movements, increasing surveillance.

Scene 2: Internal rupture
Guideline Purpose:
Highlight emotional strain, regret, fear, or conflict with allies.
Dracula Example:
Harker breaks down emotionally, realizing escape may cost him his life.

Chapter Eleven: Crisis Approaches

Purpose of the Chapter
A loss or major setback pushes the protagonist toward their lowest point.

Scene 1: Loss or setback
Guideline Purpose:
Something important is damaged, lost, or threatened.
Dracula Example:
Harker discovers Dracula has left the castle, leaving him isolated with even fewer options.

Scene 2: The world closes in
Guideline Purpose:
Multiple obstacles converge, overwhelming the protagonist.
Dracula Example:
Harker hears the vampire brides moving freely and realizes his time is nearly up.

Chapter Twelve: Preparing for the Breaking Point

Purpose of the Chapter
The protagonist reflects, regroups, and forms a bold new plan.

Scene 1: Protagonist reflects
Guideline Purpose:
This scene shows introspection, realization, or emotional clarity.
Dracula Example:
Harker writes a final journal entry accepting that he must attempt escape regardless of the danger.

Scene 2: New plan forms
Guideline Purpose:
Show a decisive plan or strategy emerging.
Dracula Example:
Harker resolves to climb the castle wall despite the risk.

Chapter Thirteen: The Crisis (All Is Lost Moment)

Purpose of the Chapter
The protagonist faces their most devastating moment.

Scene 1: The most painful moment
Guideline Purpose:
Show the protagonist hitting bottom emotionally or materially.
Dracula Example:
Harker attempts escape but is injured or nearly caught.

Scene 2: Response to the crisis
Guideline Purpose:
The protagonist confronts a truth or fear that begins internal transformation.
Dracula Example:
Harker realizes that if he is to survive, he must abandon fear completely.

Chapter Fourteen: Commitment to Final Action

Purpose of the Chapter
The protagonist regains resolve and moves toward the climax.

Scene 1: Acceptance and resolve
Guideline Purpose:
The protagonist chooses to act with determination.
Dracula Example:
Harker steels himself for one final escape attempt.

Scene 2: Moving toward climax
Guideline Purpose:
The protagonist prepares or takes first steps toward the final confrontation.
Dracula Example:
He gathers limited resources and positions himself for escape at dawn.

Chapter Fifteen: Entering the Final Conflict

Purpose of the Chapter
The protagonist enters the confrontation that will define the story's outcome.

Scene 1: The last push
Guideline Purpose:
Show the protagonist stepping fully into danger or conflict.
Dracula Example:
Harker climbs the castle walls and sees no return possible.

Scene 2: The confrontation begins
Guideline Purpose:
Initial clash or struggle starts.
Dracula Example:
He encounters supernatural obstacles or final resistance.

Chapter Sixteen: The Climax

Purpose of the Chapter
The central conflict reaches its peak; the protagonist faces the defining challenge.

Scene 1: Confronting the core obstacle
Guideline Purpose:
The protagonist uses everything learned to face the main threat.
Dracula Example:
Harker makes a final attempt to escape or defeat the immediate danger.

Scene 2: The outcome
Guideline Purpose:
The conflict resolves, revealing victory, loss, or transformation.
Dracula Example:
Harker achieves freedom or narrowly survives.

Chapter Seventeen: Aftermath

Purpose of the Chapter
Characters respond to the climax and the world begins to reset.

Scene 1: Immediate consequences
Guideline Purpose:
Show reactions, recovery, or initial settlement.
Dracula Example:
Harker awakens later in a monastery after being rescued.

Scene 2: Subplots and loose ends
Guideline Purpose:
Reveal what remains unresolved and how relationships shift.
Dracula Example:
Harker learns what has occurred in his absence, linking to later story developments.

Chapter Eighteen: Final Resolution

Purpose of the Chapter
Show the new normal and reinforce the protagonist's transformation.

Scene 1: The new normal
Guideline Purpose:
Demonstrate how life has changed after the conflict.
Dracula Example:
Harker reflects on his experience with newfound resilience.

Scene 2: Final image
Guideline Purpose:
A symbolic or emotional closing moment completes the arc.
Dracula Example:
Harker writes a final journal entry showing he will never ignore danger again.

Step 3B: Scenes in the Hero's Journey

Using the Hero's Journey Complete Guideline as the structure, with brief examples from **Alice's Adventures in Wonderland** only as illustration.

As before, the guideline determines the chapter and scene purposes. The Alice examples simply demonstrate how a writer might imagine such scene types.
Scene counts remain flexible (1–3 per chapter), depending on clarity and purpose.

Chapter One: The Hero in Their Normal Life

Purpose of the Chapter
Show the protagonist's ordinary world, their routine, and hints that something is lacking.

Scene 1: Daily life
Guideline Purpose:
Reveal the hero's typical environment and habits. Highlight what feels ordinary or repetitive.
Alice Example:
Alice sits with her sister, bored by a dry lesson and looking for amusement.

Scene 2: Demonstrate character traits
Guideline Purpose:
Show the hero's strengths, flaws, or desires through a small problem or choice.
Alice Example:
Alice follows a rabbit out of curiosity, showing impulsiveness and imagination.

Chapter Two: Establishing the Hero's Relationships

Purpose of the Chapter
Introduce important relationships and emotional anchors that will matter later.

Scene 1: Interactions with key people
Guideline Purpose:
Show bonds, tensions, or dynamics in the hero's life.
Alice Example:
Alice attempts to talk with her sister, who pays little attention, emphasizing Alice's loneliness.

Scene 2: A moment of personal reflection
Guideline Purpose:
Give the hero a quiet moment to reveal wants, fears, or dissatisfaction.
Alice Example:
Alice daydreams about a world where books have pictures, hinting at her desire for wonder.

Chapter Three: The Call Appears

Purpose of the Chapter
Introduce the event or discovery that disrupts the hero's ordinary world.

Scene 1: Introduction of the problem
Guideline Purpose:
Present something unexpected that demands attention.
Alice Example:
Alice sees the White Rabbit checking a pocket watch and realizes he is late for something important.

Scene 2: Immediate reaction
Guideline Purpose:
The hero considers or reacts to the new event with confusion, excitement, or reluctance.
Alice Example:
Alice runs after the rabbit, driven by curiosity and instinct rather than logic.

Chapter Four: The Hero Hesitates

Purpose of the Chapter
Show the hero's reluctance to commit fully to the adventure.

Scene 1: Hero avoids action
Guideline Purpose:
The hero hesitates or rationalizes reasons not to pursue the call.
Alice Example:
Alice hesitates at the rabbit hole, unsure whether to continue forward.

Scene 2: Pressure increases
Guideline Purpose:
Something worsens or becomes urgent, making refusal harder.
Alice Example:
The rabbit rushes away again, making Alice feel she must follow before the opportunity disappears.

Chapter Five: The Mentor Arrives

Purpose of the Chapter
Introduce a figure or symbol that provides insight, guidance, or direction.

Scene 1: First encounter
Guideline Purpose:
Present the mentor character or moment of guidance.
Alice Example:
Alice meets a talking creature (like the Mouse) who explains the rules of the strange environment.

Scene 2: Guidance or teaching
Guideline Purpose:
The mentor offers clarity, advice, or a tool the hero will need.
Alice Example:
The mouse tells Alice how to reach shore or how the creatures behave in Wonderland.

Chapter Six: Hero Leaves the Ordinary World

Purpose of the Chapter
Show the protagonist making the irreversible step into the adventure.

Scene 1: Decision to go
Guideline Purpose:
The hero chooses the path forward and embraces the new world.
Alice Example:
Alice chooses to drink a potion or eat a cake to proceed, symbolizing commitment.

Scene 2: First steps into the new world
Guideline Purpose:
Reveal the changes in setting, rules, or expectations.
Alice Example:
Alice shrinks or grows and must adapt quickly to the strange new reality.

Chapter Seven: The First Test

Purpose of the Chapter
Put the hero through an early challenge they are not prepared for.

Scene 1: A problem in the new world
Guideline Purpose:
Show the hero stumbling through new rules or dangers.
Alice Example:
Alice floods a room with tears and must confront the consequences of her emotions.

Scene 2: Recovery
Guideline Purpose:
The hero learns something or adjusts after the setback.
Alice Example:
Alice swims with the animals and begins to understand Wonderland social behavior.

Chapter Eight: Meeting Allies

Purpose of the Chapter
Introduce supportive characters who will help the hero navigate the new world.

Scene 1: Introduce supportive characters
Guideline Purpose:
Reveal potential allies and their value.
Alice Example:
Alice meets the Dodo and other eccentric animals.

Scene 2: Cooperation
Guideline Purpose:
Show the hero working alongside allies to achieve a small goal.
Alice Example:
Alice joins in their silly "Caucus Race," strengthening early bonds.

Chapter Nine: Facing Enemies

Purpose of the Chapter
Introduce antagonistic forces or characters who oppose the hero's progress.

Scene 1: First real confrontation
Guideline Purpose:
Show the hero struggling against an enemy or high-pressure situation.
Alice Example:
Alice argues with the Caterpillar, who confuses her and challenges her identity.

Scene 2: Narrow escape or setback
Guideline Purpose:
The hero survives but is weakened, humiliated, or uncertain.
Alice Example:
Alice follows poor advice and grows too large, causing chaos in the White Rabbit's house.

Chapter Ten: Planning for the Big Challenge

Purpose of the Chapter
Show preparation for an upcoming major ordeal.

Scene 1: Hero and allies strategize
Guideline Purpose:
The hero gathers information, strength, or resources.
Alice Example:
Alice speaks with the Cheshire Cat, who explains the layout of Wonderland and key figures like the Queen.

Scene 2: A complication arises
Guideline Purpose:
Disrupt the preparation and force adaptation.
Alice Example:
The Cat disappears abruptly, leaving Alice unsure about the next direction.

Chapter Eleven: The Major Crisis

Purpose of the Chapter
The hero faces a large-scale threat or emotional low point.

Scene 1: Enter the dangerous situation
Guideline Purpose:
Show the protagonist confronting the central threat.
Alice Example:
Alice arrives at the Queen's garden and immediately faces hostility.

Scene 2: Crisis peaks
Guideline Purpose:
The hero suffers a symbolic or emotional blow.
Alice Example:
Alice is accused in the trial, placing her future in danger.

Chapter Twelve: Gaining the Reward

Purpose of the Chapter
After surviving the crisis, the hero gains insight, strength, or a tool that changes their direction.

Scene 1: Aftermath of the ordeal
Guideline Purpose:
Show recovery or realization after the crisis.
Alice Example:
Alice questions the rules and begins standing up for herself.

Scene 2: Understanding the reward
Guideline Purpose:
Explain how the newfound knowledge or confidence alters the hero's belief.
Alice Example:
Alice grows emotionally, realizing Wonderland's authority is absurd and can be challenged.

Chapter Thirteen: Consequences of Victory

Purpose of the Chapter
Show how the world reacts to the hero's progress and how threats rise again.

Scene 1: World reacts to the ordeal
Guideline Purpose:
Reveal backlash or ripples from the hero's progress.
Alice Example:
The court becomes more chaotic and unhinged after Alice's defiance.

Scene 2: Hero moves toward final conflict
Guideline Purpose:
Build anticipation for the final confrontation.
Alice Example:
Alice demands fair treatment, pushing the tension to its peak.

Chapter Fourteen: Final Confrontation

Purpose of the Chapter
The hero must face the ultimate test that determines the story's outcome.

Scene 1: The ultimate battle
Guideline Purpose:
Show the protagonist confronting the final antagonist.
Alice Example:
Alice refuses to obey the Queen's commands during the trial.

Scene 2: True transformation
Guideline Purpose:
Show how the protagonist rises or sacrifices to complete the journey.
Alice Example:
Alice grows to full size and asserts her identity confidently.

Chapter Fifteen: Returning Home Changed

Purpose of the Chapter
Show the hero re-entering the ordinary world with newfound wisdom or identity.

Scene 1: Hero re-enters the ordinary world
Guideline Purpose:
Reveal contrast between the changed hero and unchanged world.
Alice Example:
Alice wakes up beside her sister.

Scene 2: Sharing the elixir
Guideline Purpose:
Show the hero bringing back insight or clarity.
Alice Example:
Alice reflects on her adventure and carries forward her expanded imagination.

Chapter Sixteen: The Story Closes

Purpose of the Chapter

Tie up loose emotional threads and present the final image of the hero's growth.

Scene 1: Loose ends resolved

Guideline Purpose:

Clarify remaining questions or relationships.

Alice Example:

Alice explains her dream-world experiences.

Scene 2: Final moment

Guideline Purpose:

Close with a symbolic or emotional note that reflects transformation.

Alice Example:

Alice walks off with new confidence and curiosity.

Step 3C: Scenes in Save the Cat

Using the Save the Cat Complete Guideline, with **A Christmas Carol** for all examples.

Like before, the guideline defines **chapter and scene purposes**. A Christmas Carol examples are **short**, only illustrating how a writer might imagine these scenes.

Save the Cat uses **15 beats**, which in your guideline convert to **15 chapters**.
We will follow that structure.

Chapter One: Opening Image

Purpose of the Chapter
Show the initial snapshot of the protagonist's life. This image contrasts with the final image at the end.

Scene 1: Establish the opening situation
Guideline Purpose:
Reveal the protagonist's emotional state, environment, and flaws in a single clear moment.
A Christmas Carol Example:
Scrooge rejects charity collectors, showing his coldness and isolation.

Scene 2: Reinforce the baseline
Guideline Purpose:
Add one more moment that confirms the protagonist's starting point.
A Christmas Carol Example:
Scrooge warns Cratchit about holiday cheer, showing rigidity.

Chapter Two: Theme Stated

Purpose of the Chapter
A secondary character states the story's theme. The protagonist rejects or ignores it.

Scene 1: Theme stated by someone else
Guideline Purpose:
Deliver the thematic truth the protagonist must learn.
A Christmas Carol Example:
Fred tells Scrooge that kindness brings joy, not profit.

Scene 2: Protagonist disregards the theme
Guideline Purpose:
Show the protagonist resisting growth.
A Christmas Carol Example:
Scrooge mocks Fred and refuses dinner.

Chapter Three: Set Up

Purpose of the Chapter
Expand the protagonist's world, relationships, and flaws before the catalyst arrives.

Scene 1: Display routine
Guideline Purpose:
Show daily life in more detail.
A Christmas Carol Example:
Scrooge inspects business records obsessively.

Scene 2: Introduce supporting characters
Guideline Purpose:
Present people who will matter later.
A Christmas Carol Example:
Cratchit warms his hands by the candle while waiting for release.

Chapter Four: Catalyst

Purpose of the Chapter
Introduce the disruptive event that breaks the protagonist's old life.

Scene 1: The major disruption
Guideline Purpose:
Present a surprising event that cannot be ignored.
A Christmas Carol Example:
Marley's ghost appears at Scrooge's home.

Scene 2: Immediate reaction
Guideline Purpose:
Show denial, fear, shock, or confusion.
A Christmas Carol Example:
Scrooge tries to explain away the vision as indigestion.

Chapter Five: Debate

Purpose of the Chapter
The protagonist hesitates, weighing old habits against the possibility of change.

Scene 1: Internal conflict
Guideline Purpose:
The hero debates what the catalyst means.
A Christmas Carol Example:
Scrooge locks himself inside and tries to reassure himself.

Scene 2: External pressure
Guideline Purpose:
Something pushes the protagonist toward action.
A Christmas Carol Example:
The chains on Marley shake violently, forcing Scrooge to pay attention.

Chapter Six: Break Into Two

Purpose of the Chapter
The protagonist crosses into the "new world."

Scene 1: Crossing the threshold
Guideline Purpose:
A decisive shift from old life into Act Two.
A Christmas Carol Example:
Scrooge is taken by the Ghost of Christmas Past, leaving his comfort zone.

Scene 2: First steps in the new world
Guideline Purpose:
Show the unfamiliarity of the new environment.
A Christmas Carol Example:
Scrooge sees his childhood, confused and emotional.

Chapter Seven: B Story

Purpose of the Chapter
Introduce the emotional or thematic support character.

Scene 1: Appearance of B Story figure
Guideline Purpose:
This figure represents the theme or emotional growth.
A Christmas Carol Example:
Young Scrooge's sister Fan appears, representing compassion.

Scene 2: Thematic influence
Guideline Purpose:
The hero gains insight—unwanted at first—from this figure.
A Christmas Carol Example:
Fan's kindness contrasts Scrooge's current nature.

Chapter Eight: Fun and Games

Purpose of the Chapter
Show the exploration of the new world. The "promise of the premise."

Scene 1: Exploration
Guideline Purpose:
Allow the protagonist to observe new experiences.
A Christmas Carol Example:
Scrooge watches Fezziwig's joyful Christmas party.

Scene 2: Emotional discovery
Guideline Purpose:
The protagonist experiences feelings they've ignored.
A Christmas Carol Example:
Scrooge feels nostalgia and sorrow for lost opportunities.

Chapter Nine: Midpoint

Purpose of the Chapter
A major revelation or emotional turning point. Stakes rise dramatically.

Scene 1: Major shift
Guideline Purpose:
Change the storyline's direction.
A Christmas Carol Example:
Scrooge witnesses Belle ending their engagement.

Scene 2: Hero becomes more active
Guideline Purpose:
The protagonist understands consequences more deeply.
A Christmas Carol Example:
Scrooge tries to reach out emotionally but cannot alter the past.

Chapter Ten: Bad Guys Close In

Purpose of the Chapter
Internal and external pressures intensify.

Scene 1: Rising pressure
Guideline Purpose:

Reveal consequences of resistance or failure.
A Christmas Carol Example:
The Ghost of Christmas Present shows hardship in Cratchit's home.

Scene 2: Emotional decline
Guideline Purpose:
Show the protagonist weakening or doubting.
A Christmas Carol Example:
Scrooge sees Tiny Tim's frailty and becomes fearful.

Chapter Eleven: All Is Lost

Purpose of the Chapter
A devastating moment hits the protagonist.

Scene 1: Crushing blow
Guideline Purpose:
Show the worst-case scenario.
A Christmas Carol Example:
Scrooge sees that Tiny Tim will die.

Scene 2: Emotional collapse
Guideline Purpose:
The protagonist's old beliefs break.
A Christmas Carol Example:
Scrooge cries openly, overwhelmed by guilt.

Chapter Twelve: Dark Night of the Soul

Purpose of the Chapter
The protagonist withdraws and reflects on their failures.

Scene 1: Internal collapse
Guideline Purpose:
Show introspection at the lowest point.

A Christmas Carol Example:
Scrooge asks if these visions are inevitable.

    Scene 2: Moment before breakthrough
Guideline Purpose:
A quiet moment that signals readiness for transformation.
A Christmas Carol Example:
Scrooge whispers that he wants to change.

Chapter Thirteen: Break Into Three

    Purpose of the Chapter
The protagonist commits to change and takes action.

    Scene 1: Decision
Guideline Purpose:
The hero chooses growth.
A Christmas Carol Example:
Scrooge accepts the Ghost of Christmas Yet to Come.

    Scene 2: New resolve
Guideline Purpose:
Hero prepares for the final challenge.
A Christmas Carol Example:
Scrooge follows the ghost willingly, showing courage.

Chapter Fourteen: Finale

    Purpose of the Chapter
The protagonist applies everything learned and resolves the central conflict.

    Scene 1: Confrontation
Guideline Purpose:
Hero takes action to change their destiny.
A Christmas Carol Example:
Scrooge watches people celebrating his death with relief.

Scene 2: Triumph through transformation
Guideline Purpose:
Hero overcomes the core problem through personal change.
A Christmas Carol Example:
Scrooge begs for another chance, fully transformed.

Chapter Fifteen: Final Image

Purpose of the Chapter
A final picture of the hero's new life.

Scene 1: The new self
Guideline Purpose:
Show the protagonist changed, contrasted with the opening image.
A Christmas Carol Example:
Scrooge awakens joyful and generous.

Scene 2: Final emotional note
Guideline Purpose:
Show lasting transformation and hope.
A Christmas Carol Example:
Scrooge spends Christmas with Fred and supports the Cratchits.

Step 3D: Scenes in Freytag's Pyramid

Using the Freytag's Pyramid Complete Guideline as structure, with consistent examples from **Frankenstein**.

Freytag's Pyramid divides the story into five major movements: exposition, rising action, climax, falling action, and denouement. Your guideline distributes these across **14 chapters**. As always, the guideline determines the scene purposes, and Frankenstein examples exist only to illustrate the type of scene a reader might imagine.

We will follow the same format:

Chapter Purpose

Scene 1 (Guideline Purpose + Frankenstein example)

Scene 2 (Guideline Purpose + Frankenstein example)

Scene 3 if needed

Chapter One: Exposition Begins

Purpose of the Chapter
Introduce the setting, atmosphere, and narrative frame. Ground the reader in the world before the conflict begins.

Scene 1: Establish setting and tone
Guideline Purpose:
Present the environment and initial impression of the world.
Frankenstein Example:
Walton describes the icy landscape during his voyage, setting a tone of isolation.

Scene 2: Introduce narrative frame
Guideline Purpose:
Place the reader inside the story's structural frame.
Frankenstein Example:
Walton writes letters to his sister, explaining his ambitions.

Chapter Two: Protagonist Introduced

Purpose of the Chapter
Present the protagonist and their ordinary circumstances.

Scene 1: Initial appearance
Guideline Purpose:
Introduce the protagonist through action or observation.
Frankenstein Example:
Victor begins narrating his childhood, revealing his early personality.

Scene 2: Foundation of values
Guideline Purpose:
Show what the protagonist cares about or fears.
Frankenstein Example:
Victor describes his love of learning and fascination with natural philosophy.

Chapter Three: Hint of Conflict

Purpose of the Chapter
Subtle hints appear that signal the future rise of conflict.

Scene 1: Small disturbance
Guideline Purpose:
Introduce early tension or imbalance.
Frankenstein Example:
Victor witnesses a lightning storm that inspires his fascination with electricity.

Scene 2: Growing curiosity
Guideline Purpose:
Protagonist's interest or flaw begins to push them away from stability.
Frankenstein Example:
He becomes obsessed with uncovering forbidden knowledge.

Chapter Four: Rising Action Begins

Purpose of the Chapter
The protagonist takes intentional steps toward the eventual conflict.

Scene 1: First major action
Guideline Purpose:
The protagonist commits to a path that will have consequences later.
Frankenstein Example:
Victor begins intensive scientific study at the university.

Scene 2: Early consequences
Guideline Purpose:
Show early strain or emotional cost.
Frankenstein Example:
Victor isolates himself from friends and family while studying.

Chapter Five: Conflict Expands

Purpose of the Chapter
The protagonist's choices deepen the conflict.

Scene 1: Progress toward danger
Guideline Purpose:
The protagonist makes significant progress that sets future danger in motion.
Frankenstein Example:
Victor gathers materials and begins building the creature.

Scene 2: Rising unease
Guideline Purpose:
Show discomfort with the path chosen.
Frankenstein Example:
Victor becomes sickly and exhausted due to his obsession.

Chapter Six: Pressure Increases

Purpose of the Chapter
Challenges grow, both internal and external.

Scene 1: Internal pressure
Guideline Purpose:
Reveal doubt, fear, or guilt rising within the protagonist.
Frankenstein Example:
Victor is disgusted by the parts he collects but continues.

Scene 2: External pressure
Guideline Purpose:
Introduce environmental or social strain.
Frankenstein Example:
Letters from home remind him of neglected obligations.

Chapter Seven: Approaching the Climax

Purpose of the Chapter
The protagonist nears a major turning point.

Scene 1: Tension builds
Guideline Purpose:
Reveal the approaching peak of conflict.
Frankenstein Example:
Victor works feverishly, sensing he is on the brink of a breakthrough.

Scene 2: Loss of balance
Guideline Purpose:
Show the protagonist losing clarity or stability.
Frankenstein Example:
Victor becomes physically and mentally unstable.

Chapter Eight: The Climax Begins

Purpose of the Chapter
The story reaches its highest point of conflict.

Scene 1: Moment of ultimate confrontation
Guideline Purpose:
The protagonist faces the central event.
Frankenstein Example:
Victor animates the creature and instantly regrets it.

Scene 2: Shock and aftermath
Guideline Purpose:
Immediate emotional fallout from the climax.
Frankenstein Example:
Victor flees in horror.

Chapter Nine: Aftermath of the Climax

Purpose of the Chapter
The protagonist struggles with consequences.

Scene 1: Immediate consequences
Guideline Purpose:
Show the fallout affecting the protagonist directly.
Frankenstein Example:
Victor falls into illness and delirium.

Scene 2: Escalation of consequences
Guideline Purpose:
Secondary effects take shape.
Frankenstein Example:
The creature disappears, creating uncertainty and fear.

Chapter Ten: Secondary Conflicts Rise

Purpose of the Chapter
Complications branch out from the main conflict.

Scene 1: New conflicts appear
Guideline Purpose:
Problems spread to other characters or subplots.

Frankenstein Example:
Victor learns of William's death.

   Scene 2: Emotional strain
Guideline Purpose:
The protagonist's guilt or fear deepens.
Frankenstein Example:
Victor suspects the creature but keeps silent.

Chapter Eleven: Momentum Toward Resolution

   Purpose of the Chapter
The story shifts toward closure, though tension remains.

   Scene 1: Active pursuit
Guideline Purpose:
Protagonist pursues a goal to resolve the conflict.
Frankenstein Example:
Victor vows to stop the creature's violence.

   Scene 2: Further complications
Guideline Purpose:
Conflicts remain or new issues arise.
Frankenstein Example:
Justine is blamed, leading to injustice.

Chapter Twelve: Falling Action Gains Speed

   Purpose of the Chapter
Loose ends begin tightening.

   Scene 1: Attempts at repair
Guideline Purpose:
Characters struggle to restore stability.
Frankenstein Example:
Victor tries to comfort his family after William's death.

Scene 2: Lingering threat
Guideline Purpose:
The antagonist's presence still looms.
Frankenstein Example:
Victor spots the creature in the mountains.

Chapter Thirteen: Nearing the Final Consequences

Purpose of the Chapter
The protagonist sees the long-term cost of their choices.

Scene 1: Consequences become clear
Guideline Purpose:
Show the lasting damage.
Frankenstein Example:
The creature confronts Victor and tells his story.

Scene 2: Turning point toward resolution
Guideline Purpose:
Protagonist makes a decision that determines the ending.
Frankenstein Example:
Victor reluctantly agrees to build a second creature.

Chapter Fourteen: Denouement

Purpose of the Chapter
The story concludes with reflection, clarity, and emotional closure.

Scene 1: Final settlement
Guideline Purpose:
Loose ends are resolved.
Frankenstein Example:
Victor reflects on the destruction caused by his ambition.

Scene 2: Final emotional image
Guideline Purpose:

Close with a meaningful note.

Frankenstein Example:

Walton records the creature's final appearance, showing regret and sorrow.

Step 3E: Scenes in the Seven Point Plot Structure

Using the Seven Point Plot Complete Guideline as structure, with consistent examples from **Treasure Island**.

This structure centers on seven turning points. Your guideline expands them into **eight chapters**, each with their own function. As before, scenes follow the guideline purposes; *Treasure Island* examples simply illustrate how a writer might imagine these scenes.

Scene counts remain flexible: 1–3 depending on the chapter's purpose.

Chapter One: The Hook

Purpose of the Chapter
Present the protagonist's starting point. Show what is lacking or imbalanced in their life.

Scene 1: Show the hero's current situation
Guideline Purpose:
Reveal the environment, emotional condition, and expectations the hero begins with.
Treasure Island Example:
Jim Hawkins works at the family inn, living a quiet but unsatisfying life.

Scene 2: Reveal flaw or longing
Guideline Purpose:
Show what the protagonist wants or what is missing.
Treasure Island Example:
Jim longs for adventure beyond the inn's walls.

Chapter Two: First Plot Point

Purpose of the Chapter
A major shift forces the protagonist into the main story.

Scene 1: The disruptive event
Guideline Purpose:
Introduce something that changes the hero's direction and begins the central conflict.
Treasure Island Example:
Billy Bones dies, leaving Jim with the mysterious map.

Scene 2: First reaction
Guideline Purpose:
Show the protagonist responding emotionally or practically to the disruption.
Treasure Island Example:
Jim takes the map to Dr. Livesey and Squire Trelawney.

Chapter Three: First Pinch Point

Purpose of the Chapter
Pressure increases. The antagonist or danger becomes clearer.

Scene 1: Reveal external threat
Guideline Purpose:
Show a danger or opposing force applying tension.
Treasure Island Example:
Jim overhears pirates planning to seize the treasure.

Scene 2: Hero feels pressure
Guideline Purpose:
Demonstrate how the protagonist reacts to the rising threat.
Treasure Island Example:
Jim realizes the journey will be far more dangerous than expected.

Chapter Four: Midpoint

Purpose of the Chapter
A major turning point shifts the hero's understanding.

Scene 1: Revelation or shift
Guideline Purpose:
Provide new information or clarity that changes the direction of the story.
Treasure Island Example:
Jim hides in an apple barrel and overhears that Long John Silver is leading a mutiny.

Scene 2: Hero becomes more active
Guideline Purpose:
Show the protagonist taking more purposeful action.
Treasure Island Example:
Jim alerts Captain Smollett and begins acting strategically.

Chapter Five: Second Pinch Point

Purpose of the Chapter
Threat intensifies. Stakes rise sharply.

Scene 1: Antagonist gains ground
Guideline Purpose:
Highlight growing danger and loss of control.
Treasure Island Example:
The pirates seize part of the ship and strengthen their position.

Scene 2: Hero struggles
Guideline Purpose:
Show the protagonist dealing with emotional or physical strain.
Treasure Island Example:
Jim fears the pirates may outnumber and outmatch the loyal crew.

Chapter Six: Second Plot Point

Purpose of the Chapter
The final piece of information or motivation pushes the hero toward the climax.

Scene 1: Discovery or insight
Guideline Purpose:

Introduce an element that prepares the protagonist for the final confrontation.
Treasure Island Example:
Jim discovers Ben Gunn and learns crucial information about the treasure's location.

Scene 2: Renewed determination
Guideline Purpose:
Show the protagonist committing to decisive action.
Treasure Island Example:
Jim resolves to confront Silver's crew despite the risk.

Chapter Seven: Resolution

Purpose of the Chapter
Resolve the central conflict through action and transformation.

Scene 1: Final confrontation
Guideline Purpose:
The protagonist takes action that determines the outcome of the central conflict.
Treasure Island Example:
Jim and his allies outmaneuver the pirates.

Scene 2: Outcome of the conflict
Guideline Purpose:
Show the results of the hero's actions.
Treasure Island Example:
Jim recovers the treasure and Silver escapes, defeated but alive.

Chapter Eight: Final State

Purpose of the Chapter
Show how the protagonist has changed and what the world looks like after the conflict.

Scene 1: Establish new normal
Guideline Purpose:
Show life after the journey.
Treasure Island Example:
Jim returns home with a deeper understanding of danger and adulthood.

Scene 2: Final emotional note
Guideline Purpose:
End with a moment that reflects the story's meaning.
Treasure Island Example:
Jim admits he still dreams of Silver and the sea, but with hard-won wisdom.

Activity Step 3: Adding Scenes to Your Chapters

You now have a list of plot points from Step 1 and a developing outline of chapters from Step 2. In this activity, you will continue working on those same notes. You will not start a new outline. Instead, you will expand your chapters by adding scenes beneath each one. Scenes bring your story into real time and show the specific moments where change happens.

Open the notebook, journal, tablet, or word processor where you have been building your outline. Find the chapter list you created during Step 2. Under each chapter, leave a small amount of space. You will fill this space with one to three scenes, depending on what feels natural for your story. There is no required number of scenes per chapter. Some chapters may contain a single powerful moment, while others may need two or three scenes to complete their purpose.

For each chapter, write a short description of the scene or scenes you believe belong there. Begin with the purpose of the scene, then add a brief note about the goal of the main character in that moment, the conflict or obstacle they encounter, and how the scene ends differently from how it began. Do not focus on dialogue or exact actions yet. You are only identifying the core movement of each scene.

Follow the structure you studied in Step 3. Let the examples guide you, but do not copy them. Your scenes should reflect the needs of your story and the direction of your chosen plot structure. Continue through your chapters at your own pace. Leave space beneath each scene. You will add beats in the next step.

By the end of this activity, your outline will contain plot points supported by chapters and chapters supported by scenes. You are building your story layer by layer, creating a clear path from the first idea to a full narrative structure.

Step 4: Understanding Beats

Before you begin breaking your scenes into beats, it is important to understand what beats are and how they shape your story. Beats are the smallest meaningful units of narrative movement. They are not full scenes and they are not descriptions of what generally happens. A beat captures a specific action, reaction, discovery, or emotional shift that changes the direction or momentum of the moment. When placed together, beats create the internal structure of a scene and guide the reader through the sequence of events.

A beat can be as simple as a character noticing something new, taking a small action, asking a question, or having a thought that shifts their understanding. Beats move the story forward through cause and effect. They build tension, reveal motivation, develop character, and prepare the reader for the next moment. Without beats, scenes feel flat or unclear. With them, scenes gain shape, rhythm, and purpose.

When creating beats, focus on what changes. A beat should not repeat information or restate what you have already written. Instead, each beat should mark a step in the progression of the scene. Consider the goal of the character in that moment, the obstacle they face, and the emotional or narrative shift that occurs. Beats help you see the logic of the scene and make sure every moment contributes to the chapter and to the larger structure of your story.

You will now take each scene you outlined in Step 3 and break it into beats. Keep them short. A beat is meant to be clear and functional. One to five beats per scene is typical, although the number depends on your story. Follow the structure and examples provided in this step to guide your own work.

A Note on Micro or Atomic Beats

Some writers choose to break their beats down even further into what are sometimes called micro beats or atomic beats. These are the smallest shifts within a beat, such as a glance, a pause, a brief hesitation, or a small change in tone. They capture tiny, moment-to-moment movements that shape the emotional texture of the scene.

Micro beats are useful when you want to slow the pacing, highlight tension, or draw attention to a subtle reaction. They can help you show thoughts and emotions without explaining them directly. However, they should be used carefully. Too many micro beats can make the writing feel cluttered or overly detailed. Their purpose is to enhance clarity, not to overwhelm the reader.

Use micro beats when a moment needs emphasis or when a character's internal shift is important but quiet. Add them only where they feel natural, such as before a difficult decision or during a tense exchange. If a micro beat helps the reader understand how a character feels or why they act, it has value. If it adds length without meaning, remove it. Micro beats are tools, not requirements, and they should serve the movement of the scene rather than interrupt it.

Step 4A: Beats in the Three Act Structure

Chapter One

Review the scenes for this chapter in Step 3A before filling these beats.

Scene One Beats

Beat 1: Establish setting mood (uneasy village)
Beat 2: Introduce atmosphere shift (locals fearful)
Beat 3: Early tension cue (travel warnings)

Scene Two Beats

Beat 1: Highlight character trait (Harker's professionalism)
Beat 2: Show subtle conflict (avoided answers)
Beat 3: Deepen mystery (ominous reactions)

Chapter Two

Review the scenes for this chapter in Step 3A before filling these beats.

Scene One Beats

Beat 1: Show daily routine (journal note)
Beat 2: Establish normalcy (polite conversation)
Beat 3: Hint at isolation (odd castle rules)

Scene Two Beats

Beat 1: Show small disruption (locked doors)
Beat 2: Increase suspicion (restricted movement)

Chapter Three

Review Step 3A scenes for this chapter.

Scene One Beats

Beat 1: State personal stake (career responsibility)
Beat 2: Introduce early threat (strange behavior)
Beat 3: Raise concern (unnatural sighting)

Scene Two Beats

Beat 1: Reveal limitation (no escape route)
Beat 2: Confirm danger (all exits blocked)

Chapter Four

Review Step 3A scenes.

Scene One Beats

Beat 1: Introduce major danger (vampire brides)
Beat 2: Heighten stakes (Dracula intervenes)

Scene Two Beats

Beat 1: Show emotional reaction (panic)
Beat 2: Push into next act (attempt escape)

Chapter Five

Review Step 3A scenes.

Scene One Beats

Beat 1: Enter unfamiliar territory (exploring halls)
Beat 2: Show rule shift (impossible architecture)

Scene Two Beats

Beat 1: First real conflict (locked forbidden room)
Beat 2: Foreshadow danger (disturbing evidence)

Chapter Six

Review Step 3A scenes.

Scene One Beats

Beat 1: Attempt first plan (secret letters)
Beat 2: Show failure (letters intercepted)

Scene Two Beats

Beat 1: Reveal complication (no servants)
Beat 2: Deepen suspicion (strange nightly activity)

Chapter Seven

Review Step 3A scenes.

Scene One Beats

Beat 1: Introduce potential resource (maps or books)
Beat 2: Show early adaptation (studying surroundings)

Scene Two Beats

Beat 1: Form early plan (map escape route)
Beat 2: Strengthen resolve (first confidence)

Chapter Eight

Review Step 3A scenes.

Scene One Beats

Beat 1: Increase external threat (superhuman strength)
Beat 2: Conflict escalates (danger is undeniable)

Scene Two Beats

Beat 1: Reveal inner struggle (fear blocks action)
Beat 2: Emotional shift (loss of hope)

Chapter Nine

Review Step 3A scenes.

Scene One Beats

Beat 1: Midpoint revelation (plan to travel to England)
Beat 2: Raise global stakes (threat widens)

Scene Two Beats

Beat 1: Renewed determination (escape to warn others)
Beat 2: Strategic shift (active mindset)

Chapter Ten

Review Step 3A scenes.

Scene One Beats

Beat 1: Pressure increases (Dracula watches closely)
Beat 2: Options shrink (he cannot move freely)

Scene Two Beats

Beat 1: Internal collapse (fear overwhelms him)
Beat 2: Emotional conflict (despair rises)

Chapter Eleven

Review Step 3A scenes.

Scene One Beats

Beat 1: Major setback (Dracula vanishes)
Beat 2: Uncertainty increases (loss of control)

Scene Two Beats

Beat 1: Threat closes in (brides roam freely)
Beat 2: Countdown to danger (urgency intensifies)

Chapter Twelve

Review Step 3A scenes.

Scene One Beats

Beat 1: Reflection moment (journal entry)
Beat 2: Facing truth (accepting risk)

Scene Two Beats

Beat 1: Plan formation (escape decision)
Beat 2: Resolve strengthens (fear replaced by action)

Chapter Thirteen

Review Step 3A scenes.

Scene One Beats

Beat 1: Breaking point (failed escape)
Beat 2: Emotional collapse (darkest moment)

Scene Two Beats

Beat 1: Confront inner fear (accept mortality)
Beat 2: Begin transformation (new courage forms)

Chapter Fourteen

Review Step 3A scenes.

Scene One Beats

Beat 1: Accept challenge (final resolve)
Beat 2: Emotional shift (calm determination)

Scene Two Beats

Beat 1: Move toward climax (prepare tools)
Beat 2: Act decisively (position for escape)

Chapter Fifteen

Review Step 3A scenes.

Scene One Beats

Beat 1: Step into danger (climb wall)
Beat 2: Face obstacles (supernatural interference)

Scene Two Beats

Beat 1: Begin confrontation (fight for survival)
Beat 2: Tension escalates (no turning back)

Chapter Sixteen

Review Step 3A scenes.

Scene One Beats

Beat 1: Confront primary threat (direct conflict)
Beat 2: Use learned strength (apply growth)

Scene Two Beats

Beat 1: Outcome emerges (escape succeeds)
Beat 2: New self forms (fear transforms to resolve)

Chapter Seventeen

Review Step 3A scenes.

Scene One Beats

Beat 1: Show aftermath (injury or recovery)
Beat 2: Consequences appear (story fallout)

Scene Two Beats

Beat 1: Loose ends surface (new information)
Beat 2: Prepare for closure (calm reflection)

Chapter Eighteen

Review Step 3A scenes.

Scene One Beats

Beat 1: Show new normal (life regained)
Beat 2: Character growth visible (confidence)

Scene Two Beats

Beat 1: Final thematic note (wisdom gained)
Beat 2: Closing image (changed perspective)

Step 4B: Beats in the Hero's Journey

Using Alice's Adventures in Wonderland for brief example labels (Beats ONLY — review Step 3B scenes before filling these in)

Chapter One

Review the scenes for this chapter in Step 3B before filling these beats.

Scene One Beats

Beat 1: Show normal life (bored lesson)
Beat 2: Reveal dissatisfaction (seeking amusement)

Scene Two Beats

Beat 1: Show character trait (curiosity)
Beat 2: Small disruption (rabbit sighting)

Chapter Two

Review Step 3B scenes.

Scene One Beats

Beat 1: Show relationship dynamic (sister distant)
Beat 2: Build emotional context (loneliness)

Scene Two Beats

Beat 1: Show longing (wanting picture books)
Beat 2: Character reflection (desire for wonder)

Chapter Three

Review Step 3B.

Scene One Beats

Beat 1: Present call (White Rabbit)
Beat 2: Spark curiosity (rabbit's urgency)

Scene Two Beats

Beat 1: First reaction (running after rabbit)
Beat 2: Sense of possibility (adventure starts)

Chapter Four

Review Step 3B.

Scene One Beats

Beat 1: Hero hesitates (pauses at rabbit hole)
Beat 2: Internal conflict (uncertainty)

Scene Two Beats

Beat 1: Pressure increases (rabbit running away)
Beat 2: Decision builds (must follow)

Chapter Five

Review Step 3B.

Scene One Beats

Beat 1: Mentor appears (mouse encounter)
Beat 2: Guidance begins (rules explained)

Scene Two Beats

Beat 1: Gain insight (how to navigate)
Beat 2: New understanding (social rules)

Chapter Six

Review Step 3B.

Scene One Beats

Beat 1: Enter new world (drink or eat something)
Beat 2: Physical transformation (size change)

Scene Two Beats

Beat 1: Adjust to changes (navigate new form)
Beat 2: Accept adventure (commitment)

Chapter Seven

Review Step 3B.

Scene One Beats

Beat 1: Face early challenge (flood of tears)
Beat 2: Struggle with consequences (swimming)

Scene Two Beats

Beat 1: Learn something (animal interaction)
Beat 2: Regain footing (adaptation)

Chapter Eight

Review Step 3B.

Scene One Beats

Beat 1: Meet allies (animals appear)
Beat 2: Form basic connections (conversation)

Scene Two Beats

Beat 1: Cooperation (race begins)
Beat 2: Shared moment (end of race)

Chapter Nine

Review Step 3B.

Scene One Beats

Beat 1: First enemy appears (Caterpillar challenge)
Beat 2: Conflict escalates (identity confusion)

Scene Two Beats

Beat 1: Problem worsens (size issue)
Beat 2: Escape moment (leave chaotic house)

Chapter Ten

Review Step 3B.

Scene One Beats

Beat 1: Prepare strategy (Cheshire Cat guidance)
Beat 2: Clarify direction (learn about Queen)

Scene Two Beats

Beat 1: Complication interrupts (cat vanishes)
Beat 2: Reassess path (choose direction alone)

Chapter Eleven

Review Step 3B.

Scene One Beats

Beat 1: Enter danger (Queen's garden)
Beat 2: Conflict intensifies (hostility)

Scene Two Beats

Beat 1: Accusation (trial begins)
Beat 2: Heightened stakes (risk rises)

Chapter Twelve

Review Step 3B.

Scene One Beats

Beat 1: Recover from ordeal (reflect)
Beat 2: Emotional insight (see consequences)

Scene Two Beats

Beat 1: Understand reward (inner growth)
Beat 2: New confidence (clarity)

Chapter Thirteen

Review Step 3B.

Scene One Beats

Beat 1: World reacts (trial escalates)
Beat 2: Tension builds (chaos increases)

Scene Two Beats

Beat 1: Hero moves forward (challenge authority)
Beat 2: Nearing final conflict (decision made)

Chapter Fourteen

Review Step 3B.

Scene One Beats

Beat 1: Final confrontation (stand against Queen)
Beat 2: Direct challenge (refuse commands)

Scene Two Beats

Beat 1: Transformation visible (full confidence)
Beat 2: Turning point (Queen loses power)

Chapter Fifteen

Review Step 3B.

Scene One Beats

Beat 1: Return moment (wake up)
Beat 2: Contrast worlds (ordinary life returns)

Scene Two Beats

Beat 1: Share insight (talk with sister)
Beat 2: Internal shift (growth remains)

Chapter Sixteen

Review Step 3B.

Scene One Beats

Beat 1: Resolve loose ends (reflection)
Beat 2: Emotional closure (peace)

Scene Two Beats

Beat 1: Final image (new perspective)
Beat 2: End note (lasting change)

Step 4C: Beats in Save the Cat

Chapter One: Opening Image

Review the scenes for this chapter in Step 3C before filling these beats.

Scene One Beats

Beat 1: Show who protagonist is now (cold behavior)
Beat 2: Show emotional baseline (rejects kindness)

Scene Two Beats

Beat 1: Reinforce flaw (scolds Cratchit)
Beat 2: Confirm unchanged state (rejects cheer)

Chapter Two: Theme Stated

Review Step 3C scenes.

Scene One Beats

Beat 1: Theme delivered (Fred's message)
Beat 2: Hero rejects idea (dismisses joy)

Scene Two Beats

Beat 1: Strengthen contrast (Fred's warmth)
Beat 2: Show resistance (Scrooge mocks dinner invite)

Chapter Three: Set Up

Review Step 3C.

Scene One Beats

Beat 1: Show routine (business focus)
Beat 2: Highlight flaw (obsession with money)

Scene Two Beats

Beat 1: Introduce supporting characters (Cratchit gentle)
Beat 2: Reveal dynamic (power imbalance)

Chapter Four: Catalyst

Review Step 3C.

Scene One Beats

Beat 1: Introduce life-changing event (Marley appears)
Beat 2: Create shock (ghostly warning)

Scene Two Beats

Beat 1: Hero reacts with denial (blames food)
Beat 2: Hint truth (chains rattle)

Chapter Five: Debate

Review Step 3C.

Scene One Beats

Beat 1: Hero questions event (uncertain)
Beat 2: Struggle to accept possibility (tries to rationalize)

Scene Two Beats

Beat 1: Pressure rises (Marley insists)
Beat 2: Decision point builds (hard to refuse)

Chapter Six: Break Into Two

Review Step 3C.

Scene One Beats

Beat 1: Enter new world (visits past)
Beat 2: Hero unprepared (emotional shock)

Scene Two Beats

Beat 1: Explore new environment (childhood scenes)
Beat 2: Shift perspective begins (reflective)

Chapter Seven: B Story

Review Step 3C.

Scene One Beats

Beat 1: Introduce emotional teacher (Fan appears)
Beat 2: Express theme (kindness matters)

Scene Two Beats

Beat 1: Connect emotionally (family bond)
Beat 2: Contrast with current self (lost warmth)

Chapter Eight: Fun and Games

Review Step 3C.

Scene One Beats

Beat 1: Explore lighter memories (Fezziwig joy)
Beat 2: Positive emotional shift (nostalgia)

Scene Two Beats

Beat 1: Show contrast to present (generosity)
Beat 2: Hero feels loss (regret stirs)

Chapter Nine: Midpoint

Review Step 3C.

Scene One Beats

Beat 1: Big emotional moment (Belle's decision)
Beat 2: Realization hits (love lost)

Scene Two Beats

Beat 1: Attempt correction (reaches out)
Beat 2: Accepts powerlessness (cannot change past)

Chapter Ten: Bad Guys Close In

Review Step 3C.

Scene One Beats

Beat 1: Pressure increases (Tiny Tim's condition)
Beat 2: Internal conflict rises (fear)

Scene Two Beats

Beat 1: External threat grows (future suffering)
Beat 2: Emotional strain worsens (worry for Cratchits)

Chapter Eleven: All Is Lost

Review Step 3C.

Scene One Beats

Beat 1: Worst-case revealed (Tim's death)
Beat 2: Emotional collapse (deep guilt)

Scene Two Beats

Beat 1: Lost hope (despair)
Beat 2: Realization of consequences (self-blame)

Chapter Twelve: Dark Night of the Soul

Review Step 3C.

Scene One Beats

Beat 1: Hero questions future (fear)
Beat 2: Internal break (accepts need to change)

Scene Two Beats

Beat 1: Pre-transformation moment (soft plea)
Beat 2: Emotional readiness (quiet determination)

Chapter Thirteen: Break Into Three

Review Step 3C.

Scene One Beats

Beat 1: Hero chooses change (accepts third spirit)
Beat 2: Pursues truth (goes willingly)

Scene Two Beats

Beat 1: Faces deeper fear (future shown)
Beat 2: Strength grows (resolve hardens)

Chapter Fourteen: Finale

Review Step 3C.

Scene One Beats

Beat 1: Confront final truth (reactions to death)
Beat 2: Understand impact (legacy revealed)

Scene Two Beats

Beat 1: Transformation complete (begs for chance)
Beat 2: Change affirmed (promise to reform)

Chapter Fifteen: Final Image

Review Step 3C.

Scene One Beats

Beat 1: New self-revealed (generosity)
Beat 2: Contrast to opening (warmth)

Scene Two Beats

Beat 1: Closure for relationships (celebrates with family)
Beat 2: Final emotional moment (lasting change)

Step 4D: Beats in Freytag's Pyramid

Using Frankenstein for brief example labels.
(Beats only — review Step 3D scenes before filling these in.)

Chapter One

Review the scenes for this chapter in Step 3D before filling these beats.

Scene One Beats

Beat 1: Establish setting tone (icy voyage)
Beat 2: Present narrator frame (letters)

Scene Two Beats

Beat 1: Introduce goal (Walton's ambition)
Beat 2: Hint isolation (lonely journey)

Chapter Two

Review Step 3D.

Scene One Beats

Beat 1: Introduce protagonist (Victor's childhood)
Beat 2: Reveal early traits (curiosity)

Scene Two Beats

Beat 1: Show core values (love of learning)
Beat 2: Foreshadow flaw (obsession begins)

Chapter Three

Review Step 3D.

Scene One Beats

Beat 1: Early disturbance (lightning storm)
Beat 2: Spark fascination (electricity mystery)

Scene Two Beats

Beat 1: Curiosity increases (research urge)
Beat 2: Pull away from normalcy (growing fixation)

Chapter Four

Review Step 3D.

Scene One Beats

Beat 1: Commit to study (university work)
Beat 2: Dive into knowledge (intense focus)

Scene Two Beats

Beat 1: Consequence emerges (isolation)
Beat 2: Emotional strain begins (fatigue)

Chapter Five

Review Step 3D.

Scene One Beats

Beat 1: Approach danger (gather materials)
Beat 2: Progress accelerates (building creature)

Scene Two Beats

Beat 1: Recognize unease (disgust rising)
Beat 2: Ignore intuition (push forward)

Chapter Six

Review Step 3D.

Scene One Beats

Beat 1: Internal conflict rises (self-doubt)
Beat 2: Fear grows (moral hesitation)

Scene Two Beats

Beat 1: External pressure (family letters)
Beat 2: Guilt stirs (neglected bonds)

Chapter Seven

Review Step 3D.

Scene One Beats

Beat 1: Build tension (near breakthrough)
Beat 2: Strain increases (mental instability)

Scene Two Beats

Beat 1: Lose clarity (fixation deepens)
Beat 2: Foreshadow collapse (near breaking)

Chapter Eight

Review Step 3D.

Scene One Beats

Beat 1: Moment of climax (awakening creature)
Beat 2: Shock and horror (instant regret)

Scene Two Beats

Beat 1: Immediate escape (flee room)
Beat 2: Emotional devastation (collapse)

Chapter Nine

Review Step 3D.

Scene One Beats

Beat 1: Immediate aftermath (illness)
Beat 2: Loss of control (delirium)

Scene Two Beats

Beat 1: Lingering uncertainty (creature gone)
Beat 2: Suspense rises (unknown danger)

Chapter Ten

Review Step 3D.

Scene One Beats

Beat 1: New conflict appears (William's death)
Beat 2: Emotional impact (grief)

Scene Two Beats

Beat 1: Inner conflict (suspects creature)
Beat 2: Silence choice (keeps truth hidden)

Chapter Eleven

Review Step 3D.

Scene One Beats

Beat 1: Pursue resolution (vows to stop creature)
Beat 2: Renew purpose (anger builds)

Scene Two Beats

Beat 1: Complication (Justine accused)
Beat 2: Emotional turmoil (feels responsible)

Chapter Twelve

Review Step 3D.

Scene One Beats

Beat 1: Attempt to repair (comfort family)
Beat 2: Reveal emotional damage (worry)

Scene Two Beats

Beat 1: Threat resurfaces (creature seen)
Beat 2: Renewed tension (confrontation nears)

Chapter Thirteen

Review Step 3D.

Scene One Beats

Beat 1: Face consequences (creature's story)
Beat 2: Realization (guilt deepens)

Scene Two Beats

Beat 1: Critical decision (make second creature)
Beat 2: Set direction (prepares for next step)

Chapter Fourteen

Review Step 3D.

Scene One Beats

Beat 1: Loose ends tied (reflection)
Beat 2: Emotional resolution (clarity)

Scene Two Beats

Beat 1: Final image (creature mourning)
Beat 2: Thematic closure (sorrow and regret)

Step 4E: Beats in the Seven Point Plot Structure

Using Treasure Island for short example labels.
(Beats only — review the scenes for this chapter in Step 3E before filling these in.)

The Seven Point Plot guideline expands into eight chapters. Each scene receives 1–5 beats, depending on clarity and purpose.

Chapter One: The Hook

Review the scenes for this chapter in Step 3E before filling these beats.

Scene One Beats

Beat 1: Show ordinary life (inn chores)
Beat 2: Reveal desire (craving adventure)

Scene Two Beats

Beat 1: Show flaw or vulnerability (boredom)
Beat 2: Hint future conflict (tension at inn)

Chapter Two: First Plot Point

Review Step 3E scenes.

Scene One Beats

Beat 1: Introduce disruptive event (Billy Bones dies)
Beat 2: Reveal key object (treasure map)

Scene Two Beats

Beat 1: First reaction (seeks adults' help)
Beat 2: Shift toward story (meeting Livesey)

Chapter Three: First Pinch Point

Review Step 3E scenes.

Scene One Beats

Beat 1: Show external threat (pirate plotting)
Beat 2: Increase pressure (danger overheard)

Scene Two Beats

Beat 1: Emotional tension rises (fear)
Beat 2: Stakes become clear (journey dangerous)

Chapter Four: Midpoint

Review Step 3E scenes.

Scene One Beats

Beat 1: Reveal major truth (Silver's mutiny)
Beat 2: Raise central stakes (treachery exposed)

Scene Two Beats

Beat 1: Hero becomes active (warns captain)
Beat 2: Strategic shift (prepares defense)

Chapter Five: Second Pinch Point

Review Step 3E scenes.

Scene One Beats

Beat 1: Antagonist gains ground (pirates seize control)
Beat 2: Situation worsens (outnumbered crew)

Scene Two Beats

Beat 1: Hero overwhelmed (stress increases)
Beat 2: Pressure intensifies (pirates advance)

Chapter Six: Second Plot Point

Review Step 3E scenes.

Scene One Beats

Beat 1: New discovery (Ben Gunn insight)
Beat 2: Reveal final piece of plan (treasure info)

Scene Two Beats

Beat 1: Renew resolve (Jim commits to action)
Beat 2: Prepare for climax (plans confrontation)

Chapter Seven: Resolution

Review Step 3E scenes.

Scene One Beats

Beat 1: Final confrontation begins (pirates opposed)
Beat 2: Conflict turns (crew gains control)

Scene Two Beats

Beat 1: Outcome of battle (pirates defeated)
Beat 2: Treasure secured (victory)

Chapter Eight: Final State

Review Step 3E scenes.

Scene One Beats

Beat 1: Show new normal (home return)
Beat 2: Growth visible (maturity gained)

Scene Two Beats

Beat 1: Final reflection (sea memories linger)
Beat 2: Last emotional note (wisdom earned)

Activity for Step 4: Breaking Scenes into Beats

In Step 3, you added scenes beneath each chapter. Now you will take those scenes and break them into beats. Beats are the smallest units of story movement. Each beat marks a meaningful action, reaction, decision, or shift. They build your scenes moment by moment and show exactly how the scene progresses.

Open the same notes you have been building throughout this workbook. Find the scenes you listed beneath each chapter. Under each scene, leave a small amount of space. You will now add one to five beats to that scene, depending on what the moment requires. There is no correct number. Some scenes are tight and need only one or two beats. Others unfold in several steps and benefit from more.

For each beat, write a short description that states the purpose of the moment and what changes because of it. These descriptions do not need to be long. A single sentence or phrase is often enough. If you found the beat lists in Step 4 helpful, use them as models. Look at how each beat moves the scene forward or shifts the character's emotional state. Your goal is to identify the internal structure of your scenes so they lead clearly from one chapter to the next.

Continue this process for every scene in your outline. Take your time. The purpose of this activity is not to perfect your story but to understand how it moves in small, purposeful steps. These beats will guide your writing when you begin drafting your novel. They show you the exact rhythm of your story and help you maintain clarity as you write.

When you finish, you will have a complete outline that includes plot points, chapters, scenes, and beats. This layered structure will support you through the drafting process and keep your story grounded in clear progression. If you need guidance or want to compare your work to other approaches, refer to the additional samples listed in the index at the back of this workbook.

Step 5: Turning Your Structure Into Story

You now have the full foundation of your novel. You chose a plot structure, built your chapters, broke those chapters into scenes, and shaped each scene with purposeful beats. This layered outline is your blueprint. Step 5 is where you learn how to use that blueprint to begin writing your story on the page.

Writing a novel becomes far less overwhelming when you understand how each piece supports the next. The outline you created is not just a map. It is a companion that guides you from moment to moment so you never face a blank page without direction. Step 5 will show you how to move from this structure into actual narrative writing.

The goal here is not to start drafting immediately. It is to understand how your outline transforms into usable story material. You will learn how to read your beats, how to expand them organically into prose, and how to keep the original purpose of each scene intact as you write.

Begin by reviewing your outline from the top. Look at your plot points, your chapters, and the scenes you built beneath them. Each beat already contains the seeds of action, emotion, and change. When you start drafting, those beats become individual story moments. The chapter still serves its purpose, and the scene still moves the story forward, but the beats now grow into sentences, interactions, and descriptions.

To turn structure into story, focus on the character in each moment. Beats tell you what happens and why it matters. Your task now is to express how the character experiences it. Ask how they feel, what they notice, what choice they make, and how their decision changes the direction of the moment. Emotion and reaction bring a beat to life. You are not adding new plot; you are allowing the outline to breathe.

When writing from beats, resist the urge to overthink. A beat does not require elaborate prose. It only needs to become a clear moment on the page. You may choose to write a few sentences, a paragraph, or several paragraphs depending on what the scene needs. Let the character's voice and the story's tone guide you. The outline keeps you pointed in the right direction. Your writing brings the experience to life.

As you expand your scenes, allow flexibility. Outlines guide you, but they should not restrict you. If a beat naturally flows into a different order or expands into an unexpected moment, that is part of the creative process. Do not force yourself to follow the structure rigidly. Instead, let the outline support you while giving your imagination room to move. As long as the purpose of the scene is respected, your story will stay on track.

Consider pacing as you write. Chapters that contain heavy emotional beats may benefit from quieter moments or internal reflection. Action-driven scenes may move quickly from one beat to the next. Your outline helps you anticipate these shifts. Use it to balance faster and slower moments so the story feels steady and intentional.

When you finish translating a few beats into prose, pause and read what you have written. Compare the draft to your original purpose for the scene. Ask yourself whether the outcome still matches the intention. If the answer is yes, continue. If not, adjust your writing or your outline. The outline is a living document. It can be refined as your understanding deepens.

Step 5 is where preparation becomes momentum. You are no longer planning your novel. You are building it from the inside out. With your structure in place, you are ready to write scenes with confidence, clarity, and purpose.

You will begin creating a personal guideline that supports your drafting process. This guideline will serve as your reference throughout your novel, helping you stay grounded in your plot, structure, and character progression. You now have everything you need to move forward with intention and begin turning your ideas into a full story.

As you move forward, begin shaping your own working guideline. Take the outline you built in Steps 1 through 4 and organize it into a clean document you can keep beside you as you write. Start with your chosen plot structure at the top, followed by your chapter list. Beneath each chapter, place your scenes. Under each scene, place the beats you developed. This becomes your full novel blueprint. Some writers keep this guideline in a separate notebook or digital file. Others place it in a split screen or print it out so it is always visible. Use the format that feels most natural and comfortable.

Your guideline should not feel rigid. Think of it as a living resource rather than a strict set of instructions. As you draft, you may find that a scene needs an extra beat or that a chapter could be better placed earlier or later in the story. These adjustments are part of the creative process. Return to your guideline and update it as needed. The purpose of this document is to support you, not to constrain you. Use it to stay grounded, but allow your story the flexibility it needs to grow.

When you are ready to draft, begin with one chapter at a time. Look at the first scene, read its beats, and let them guide you. Start writing the moment as it unfolds. Describe the setting, capture the character's reactions, and follow the flow of the beats naturally. Do not feel the pressure to write perfectly. Step 5 is about starting the process with clarity and confidence, not perfection. The structure ensures you always know where the story is going, even if some parts feel uncertain as you write them.

Pay attention to emotional continuity as you move between beats. A beat that shows rising tension should move into a moment where the character reacts. A beat that reveals new information should shift the scene's direction. These transitions are what make the writing feel natural. Allow each beat to lead you. Your outline gives you the order, but your draft provides the life within it.

When you reach the end of a scene, pause and confirm that the outcome reflects the intention you set in your outline. If the result matches the purpose of the scene, move on to the next. If the scene feels off, ask yourself where the beat progression may have shifted and revise as needed. These adjustments help strengthen your understanding of your story and refine your structure.

As you continue writing, your guideline may change. You may discover stronger motivations, deeper conflicts, or new emotional layers. This is expected. Writing is not a linear process. Let your discoveries shape your guideline as much as your guideline shapes your writing. Update beats when new details emerge, and adjust scenes if the story grows in unexpected ways. This balance ensures your story remains both structured and alive.

During this step, do not worry about style, grammar, or perfect pacing. Your focus should be on translating structure into narrative. You are learning how the pieces you built work together. The refinement will come later. For now, your goal is to connect your outline with your writing through steady, intentional progress.

Your guideline will become your companion throughout the drafting process. It will help you stay oriented, remind you of your goals, and keep the pacing of your story clear. Many writers rely on this document to prevent getting stuck or lost in the middle of their novels. Because you built it layer by layer, it reflects your story from the inside out. Now you can trust it to support you as you begin writing.

Use this step to practice. Choose one chapter from your outline and begin expanding its beats into a full scene. Let the process teach you how your structure moves and how your writing responds. As you grow more comfortable, move through additional chapters at your own pace. By the time you complete this phase, you will understand how to move confidently from beat to prose and chapter to chapter.

You are now prepared to take the next step toward drafting your novel. With your guideline in place and your understanding of structure fully developed, you have all the tools you need to begin writing with intention. Your story has shape, meaning, and direction. The work you have done has set the foundation for a strong first draft, ready to come to life on the page.

Three Approaches to Beginning Your Draft

As you move from structure to story, it can be helpful to choose a writing approach that matches the way your mind works. Writers tend to fall into different patterns when they draft, and each method is valid as long as the structure you built remains your guide. Below are three approaches you may use. You may adopt one, switch between them, or blend them as needed.

1. Writing at the Micro Level

This approach focuses on writing your story in the exact order of your outline, beginning with the first chapter and moving beat by beat, scene by scene. You follow the structure as it was built in Steps 1 through 4. This method is helpful if you prefer stability and direction as you write. You always know what comes next, and the outline keeps you from getting stuck or overwhelmed. Write one beat, then the next, and let the story grow naturally in the order you planned.

2. Writing at the Macro Level

This approach begins with a broad view. You start by drafting a general version of the story, moving through the chapters lightly and letting the main events unfold without worrying about the smaller details. Once the larger shape feels clear, you return to each chapter and enrich it with the scenes and beats you built in your outline. This method works well if you prefer to understand the whole arc first, then fill in depth and emotion afterward. The structure acts as a scaffold, and you gradually tighten each section until the story feels complete.

3. Using AI as a Support Tool

Some writers choose to use AI to help them expand their outline into prose. If you choose this method, treat AI as a tool, not a replacement for your imagination. You may ask it to help you improve the flow of beats, generate variations of a scene idea, or fill in descriptive details that follow your original structure. This approach should never replace your creative choices. The story must remain yours. AI is like autocorrect or a writing assistant. It can help you follow your own guideline more efficiently, but it should not invent the story for you. Use it to support your voice, not to overshadow it.

Final Thoughts and Your Next Step

You have reached the end of this workbook, but the real beginning lies ahead. You built your story layer by layer, starting with the broad movement of your plot, then shaping chapters, developing scenes, and identifying the beats that form the heart of your narrative. You learned how each piece supports the next and how a clear structure can guide your creativity rather than limit it. You now have a foundation strong enough to carry a full novel.

The next part of your journey is to take what you have created and begin writing. Whether you choose to work beat by beat, chapter by chapter, or with a wider approach that fills in details over time, you are ready. The outline you built gives you direction. The exercises you completed taught you how to break overwhelming work into manageable steps. You no longer face a blank page. You face a plan built from your own ideas.

There will still be challenges. Every writer encounters days when the words come slowly or when scenes feel difficult to shape. When that happens, return to the structure you built. Your plot points, chapters, scenes, and beats are there to steady you. They remind you where the story is going and why each moment matters. Use them to stay grounded, and let them guide you through uncertainty.

Do not wait for perfect inspiration. Writing grows from action, not hesitation. Begin with one scene. Write one moment. Let the story unfold one decision at a time. Consistency will take you farther than the search for perfection ever will. Trust the process you learned here and trust the outline you created. It is designed to help you move forward.

Your novel exists now in its full shape. All that remains is to bring it to life on the page. You have the tools, the structure, and the understanding to begin. This is the moment where planning becomes creation and where intention becomes story. Take a breath, look at your guideline, and start writing. The journey is yours, and you are ready to take the first step.

Index: Generic Samples

The Following are generic samples of different Plot types Chapter descriptions, Scenes, and Beats with descriptions.

3 ACT STRUCTURE — STANDARD CHAPTER, SCENE AND BEAT OUTLINE

ACT I: SETUP

(4 chapters, 6–10 scenes)

- **Chapter One: Introduction to the World**
  - Scene: Establish setting and tone
    - Present the environment
    - Introduce atmosphere or mood
    - Show the world at rest
  - Scene: Initial character moment
    - Introduce the protagonist
    - Reveal a defining trait
    - Suggest internal tension

- **Chapter Two: Establish the Character's Normal Life**
  - Scene: Show daily routine
    - Demonstrate habits
    - Show relationships
    - Reveal what the character values
  - Scene: Light conflict appears
    - A small disruption hints at instability
    - Protagonist reacts
    - Tone shifts toward unease

- **Chapter Three: Setting the Stakes**
  - Scene: Show what can be gained or lost

- - Personal goals become visible
  - Responsibilities or threats emerge
  - Emotional stakes rise
- Scene: Pressure increases
  - Hints of the coming conflict grow stronger
  - The protagonist is nudged toward change
  - Momentum builds

- **Chapter Four: The Inciting Incident**
- Scene: The major disruptive event
  - Something unexpected happens
  - Normal life breaks
  - Conflict becomes unavoidable
- Scene: First reaction
  - Emotional response
  - Attempts to deny or avoid
  - Movement toward Act II begins

ACT II: CONFRONTATION

(10 chapters, 15–25 scenes)
This is the longest and densest part of the story.

- **Chapter Five: First Steps into the New World**
- Scene: Entering unfamiliar territory
  - Protagonist crosses into the new situation
  - Rules have changed
  - They feel out of place
- Scene: First conflict in the new world
  - A challenge appears
  - Protagonist fails or struggles
  - Stakes rise

- **Chapter Six: Early Attempts and First Failures**
- Scene: The protagonist tries to handle the conflict
  - First plan is attempted
  - Partial or full failure
  - Pressure increases

- Scene: Reveal of new obstacles
    - Antagonistic force becomes more visible
    - Complications combine
    - Tension builds
- **Chapter Seven: Building Alliances and Resources**
- Scene: Supporting characters join
    - Allies appear
    - Trust begins forming
    - New tools or knowledge introduced
- Scene: Plan formation
    - Group outlines an approach
    - Protagonist takes leadership or struggles to
    - Hope rises
- **Chapter Eight: Rising Challenges**
- Scene: Conflict intensifies
    - Antagonistic force pushes harder
    - Protagonist must adapt
    - Emotions rise
- Scene: A deeper struggle
    - Internal conflict surfaces
    - Mistake or misjudgment occurs
    - Costs become visible
- **Chapter Nine: Midpoint Shift**
- Scene: Major event changes direction
    - A victory that feels like a loss
    - Or a defeat that changes understanding
    - Stakes escalate sharply
- Scene: Protagonist gains new clarity
    - Learns a truth or gains insight
    - Becomes more active
    - Conflict takes on new meaning
- **Chapter Ten: Turning Pressure Upward**
- Scene: External forces apply pressure
    - Enemy or obstacle grows stronger
    - Plans fail

- - Consequences deepen
- Scene: Internal rupture
  - Self-doubt or fear resurfaces
  - Relationship tension increases
  - Protagonist loses ground

- **Chapter Eleven: Crisis Approaches**
- Scene: Loss or setback
  - Something important is damaged
  - A friend, resource, or plan collapses
  - Emotional strain hits peak
- Scene: The world closes in
  - Obstacles converge
  - Protagonist feels overwhelmed
  - Crisis becomes inevitable

- **Chapter Twelve: Preparing for the Breaking Point**
- Scene: Protagonist reflects
  - Evaluates mistakes
  - Faces inner flaw
  - Finds new strength
- Scene: New plan forms
  - Allies regroup
  - A bolder strategy emerges
  - Movement toward Act III begins

- **Chapter Thirteen: The Crisis (All Is Lost Moment)**
- Scene: The most painful moment
  - Protagonist faces devastating loss
  - Something vital collapses
  - Emotion reaches lowest point
- Scene: Response to the crisis
  - They confront inner truth
  - Realization dawns
  - Transformation begins

- **Chapter Fourteen: Commitment to Final Action**
- Scene: Acceptance and resolve
  - Protagonist chooses to act

- Fear becomes determination
- Direction becomes clear
- Scene: Moving toward climax
  - Final preparations
  - Allies support or block
  - Tension builds

ACT III: RESOLUTION

(4 chapters, 6–10 scenes)

- **Chapter Fifteen: Entering the Final Conflict**
- Scene: The last push
  - Protagonist steps into confrontation
  - Forces collide
  - stakes peak
- Scene: The confrontation begins
  - Early exchange or struggle
  - Protagonist applies growth
  - Conflict escalates

- **Chapter Sixteen: The Climax**
- Scene: Confronting the core obstacle
  - The largest conflict reaches its peak
  - Protagonist uses everything learned
  - A decisive moment emerges
- Scene: The outcome
  - Victory, defeat, or bittersweet resolution
  - Emotional turning point
  - Transformation becomes visible

- **Chapter Seventeen: Aftermath**
- Scene: Immediate consequences
  - Characters respond to the climax
  - World begins to reset
  - Emotions settle
- Scene: Subplots and loose ends
  - Return to relationships

- Resolve secondary conflicts
- Show how the world shifts
- **Chapter Eighteen: Final Resolution**
  - Scene: The new normal
    - Show what life has become
    - Demonstrate character growth
    - Stability returns
  - Scene: Final image
    - A symbolic closing beat
    - Reflects the beginning
    - Story closes with clarity

HERO'S JOURNEY PLOT LINE

The Ordinary World

- **Chapter One: The Hero in Their Normal Life**
  - Scene: Daily life
    - Show the world before the adventure
    - Highlight routine and rhythms
    - Reveal something missing or unfulfilled
  - Scene: Demonstrate character traits
    - Show how the hero handles a small problem
    - Reveal strengths and flaws
    - Hint the world is about to shift
- **Chapter Two: Establishing the Hero's Relationships**
  - Scene: Interactions with key people
    - Show bonds or tensions
    - Reveal emotional anchors
    - Hint at what will be at risk later
  - Scene: A moment of personal reflection
    - The hero expresses wants or fears
    - Something symbolic appears
    - Tone shifts enough to suggest coming change

The Call to Adventure

- **Chapter Three: The Call Appears**
  - Scene: Introduction of the problem
    - A message, event, or discovery arrives
    - It disrupts routine
    - Stakes becomes faintly visible
  - Scene: Immediate reaction
    - Hero processes the call
    - Confusion or curiosity arises
    - A sense of inevitability forms

Refusal of the Call

- **Chapter Four: The Hero Hesitates**
  - Scene: Hero avoids action

- They name reasons to stay
- Fear or comfort holds them back
- Someone reinforces their reluctance
◦ Scene: Pressure increases
- The situation worsens
- Avoidance creates consequences
- The call becomes harder to ignore

Meeting the Mentor

- **Chapter Five: The Mentor Arrives**

◦ Scene: First encounter
- Mentor provides perspective
- A clue or tool appears
- Hero begins to question refusal

◦ Scene: Guidance or teaching
- Advice or training begins
- Hero gains clarity
- A spark of courage is formed

Crossing the Threshold

- **Chapter Six: Hero Leaves the Ordinary World**

◦ Scene: Decision to go
- Hero commits to the journey
- Something symbolic marks the choice
- Tension and excitement rise

◦ Scene: First steps into the new world
- Environment or situation changes
- New expectations appear
- Hero recognizes the point of no return

Tests, Allies, and Enemies

- **Chapter Seven: The First Test**

◦ Scene: A problem in the new world
- Hero faces a challenge they are not ready for
- Failure teaches them something
- Stakes are clarified

◦ Scene: Recovery

- Hero reassesses their approach
  - Gains insight from the mistake
  - Learns something about the world

- **Chapter Eight: Meeting Allies**
  ○ Scene: Introduce supportive characters
    - New allies reveal their value
    - A bond begins
    - Characters share goals or struggles
  ○ Scene: Cooperation
    - Hero works with allies on a small task
    - Trust grows
    - Group dynamic forms

- **Chapter Nine: Facing Enemies**
  ○ Scene: First real confrontation
    - Enemy or opposition emerges
    - Hero struggles
    - Conflict escalates
  ○ Scene: Narrow escape or setback
    - Hero survives but pays a cost
    - Enemy threat becomes clear
    - Tension rises

Approach to the Inmost Cave

- **Chapter Ten: Planning for the Big Challenge**
  ○ Scene: Hero and allies strategize
    - They prepare mentally or physically
    - Doubts appear
    - Stakes are restated
  ○ Scene: A complication arises
    - Preparation is disrupted
    - Hero must adapt
    - Pressure increases

The Ordeal

- **Chapter Eleven: The Major Crisis**
  ○ Scene: Enter the dangerous situation

- Hero faces the central threat
- Conflict reaches intensity
- Loss feels possible
- Scene: Crisis peaks
  - Hero suffers a symbolic or real death
  - They confront their deepest fear
  - Turning point occurs

Reward

- **Chapter Twelve: Gaining the Reward**
- Scene: Aftermath of the ordeal
  - Hero grasps what they have won
  - Recovery begins
  - Relief or confusion appears
- Scene: Understanding the reward
  - The reward changes the hero's outlook
  - New knowledge or power emerges
  - The path forward becomes visible

The Road Back

- **Chapter Thirteen: Consequences of Victory**
- Scene: World reacts to the ordeal
  - New dangers appear
  - Enemy regroups or strikes back
  - Hero feels urgency
- Scene: Hero moves toward final conflict
  - Allies prepare or divide
  - Tension heightens
  - Countdown begins

The Resurrection

- **Chapter Fourteen: Final Confrontation**
- Scene: The ultimate battle
  - Hero confronts the final threat
  - Everything learned is tested
  - Stakes reach peak intensity
- Scene: True transformation

- Hero rises, overcomes, or sacrifices
        - Identity shifts
        - Victory or loss becomes clear

Return with the Elixir

- **Chapter Fifteen: Returning Home Changed**
  - Scene: Hero re-enters the ordinary world
    - World feels different
    - Hero carries new confidence or wounds
    - People react to their change
  - Scene: Sharing the elixir
    - Hero brings back knowledge or healing
    - Community benefits
    - A new normal begins

Final Resolution

- **Chapter Sixteen: The Story Closes**
  - Scene: Loose ends resolved
    - Remaining questions answered
    - Relationships clarified
    - Stability returns
  - Scene: Final moment
    - A symbolic closing action
    - Tone settles into hope or reflection
    - Journey feels complete

SAVE THE CAT — OFFICIAL 15 BEATS WITH SCENES + BEATS

- **Chapter One: Opening Image**
  - Scene: Show the hero's everyday world
    - A visual that captures life before the story
    - A detail showing routine or normal behavior
    - A hint of what feels off or unbalanced
  - Scene: Reveal the hero as they are now
    - Show a habit or flaw
    - Present a small problem
    - Suggest inner dissatisfaction
- **Chapter Two: Theme Stated**
  - Scene: Someone speaks the story's lesson
    - A line that points toward the theme
    - Hero brushes it off
    - Reader gets a clear hint
  - Scene: Hero behaves opposite to the theme
    - They act from fear, pride, or flaw
    - Show why they reject the lesson
    - A light consequence follows
- **Chapter Three: Set Up**
  - Scene: Show hero's relationships
    - Introduce key people
    - Reveal positive and negative dynamics
    - Show what matters emotionally
  - Scene: Establish stakes
    - Show what the hero could lose
    - Present responsibilities or goals
    - Demonstrate early pressure
- **Chapter Four: Catalyst**
  - Scene: The life-changing event
    - Something arrives or happens suddenly

- Hero's normal world is hit hard
- Stability collapses
- Scene: Hero reacts
  - Emotion spikes
  - Confusion or disbelief
  - Realization that nothing is the same

- **Chapter Five: Debate**
- Scene: Hero resists change
  - Lists reasons to avoid action
  - Fear or doubt dominates
  - A push to stay comfortable
- Scene: Pressure grows
  - Life gets worse without action
  - Avoidance causes problems
  - Hero is forced toward a decision

- **Chapter Six: Break into Two**
- Scene: Hero decides
  - A choice is made
  - A symbolic moment marks the shift
  - They leave the old world
- Scene: Entering the new world
  - Environment or situation changes
  - New rules appear
  - Hero realizes there is no going back

- **Chapter Seven: B Story**
- Scene: Introduce the emotional support character
  - Could be mentor, friend, love interest, ally
  - Provide contrast to hero's worldview
  - First spark of connection
- Scene: Thematic reinforcement
  - Hero shares fears or hopes
  - Relationship strengthens
  - Theme appears subtly again

- **Chapter Eight: Fun and Games**
- Scene: Hero explores the new world

- First taste of adventure
- Early wins or interesting surprises
- Tone feels lighter
      - Scene: Contrast with old life
        - Hero begins to enjoy the change
        - Skills or confidence grow
        - Obstacles feel manageable
- **Chapter Nine: Midpoint**
  - Scene: Major shift
    - Big win or big loss
    - Stakes become clearer
    - Direction pivots sharply
  - Scene: New urgency
    - A countdown or time pressure forms
    - Enemy or obstacle activates
    - Hero must rise to the new level
- **Chapter Ten: Bad Guys Close In**
  - Scene: External problems intensify
    - Antagonists gain ground
    - Threats increase
    - Hero feels squeezed
  - Scene: Internal pressure grows
    - Doubts return
    - Relationships strain
    - Mistakes carry heavier consequences
- **Chapter Eleven: All Is Lost**
  - Scene: Devastating blow
    - Something vital is lost
    - Hero reaches their lowest point
    - Symbolic loss appears
  - Scene: Collapse begins
    - They feel alone or betrayed
    - Attempts fail completely
    - World seems to fall apart

- **Chapter Twelve: Dark Night of the Soul**
  - Scene: Emotional crisis
    - Hero feels hopeless
    - Confronts inner truth or flaw
    - Reflects on failures
  - Scene: Insight forms
    - A small realization appears
    - Theme resurfaces clearly
    - Hero finds the spark to continue
- **Chapter Thirteen: Break into Three**
  - Scene: Hero makes a new decision
    - They understand the theme
    - They gain clarity
    - A new strategy emerges
  - Scene: Step toward the finale
    - Allies regroup
    - Plan strengthens
    - Hero commits fully
- **Chapter Fourteen: Finale**
  - Scene: Execute the final plan
    - Hero applies lessons learned
    - Problems are confronted directly
    - Old flaws are overcome
  - Scene: Final confrontation
    - Conflict resolves
    - Hero rises or sacrifices
    - Story threads come together
- **Chapter Fifteen: Final Image**
  - Scene: Show the hero's new life
    - Visual contrast with Opening Image
    - Hero demonstrates change
    - World feels different
  - Scene: Last symbolic moment
    - A gesture that reflects the theme

- Emotional closure
- Clear sense of completion

FREYTAG'S PYRAMID —STRUCTURE WITH CHAPTERS, SCENES AND BEATS

Freytag's Pyramid divides a story into **five major movements**:

Exposition
Rising Action
Climax
Falling Action
Denouement

Each movement naturally varies in size. Below is the **standard professional breakdown**, using typical chapter counts in commercial fiction and proper scene-beat density.

I. EXPOSITION

(4 chapters, 6–10 scenes total)

- **Chapter One: The Ordinary World**
  - Scene: Establish setting
    - Introduce environment and tone
    - Describe social norms
    - Show the world at rest
  - Scene: Initial character presence
    - Present the protagonist
    - Show a core trait
    - Reveal emotional baseline

- **Chapter Two: Relationships and Roles**
  - Scene: Supporting cast introduction
    - Show family, friends, coworkers, or community
    - Reveal character relationships
    - Suggest existing tensions
  - Scene: Stakes preview
    - Show what the protagonist values
    - Reveal what could be threatened later
    - Foreshadow change

- **Chapter Three: Inciting Disturbance**
  ◦ Scene: First hint of trouble
    ▪ Something unusual or concerning happens
    ▪ Protagonist takes note
    ▪ Suspense increases
  ◦ Scene: Immediate consequence
    ▪ The disturbance affects someone or something
    ▪ The world loses its perfect balance
    ▪ Protagonist is unsettled

- **Chapter Four: Direction Shifts**
  ◦ Scene: Early reaction
    ▪ Protagonist struggles to maintain normalcy
    ▪ They attempt to downplay events
    ▪ Pressure builds
  ◦ Scene: Pointing toward conflict
    ▪ New information pressures the protagonist
    ▪ A dilemma begins forming
    ▪ Movement into rising action begins

II. RISING ACTION

(6 chapters, 10–18 scenes total)
This section becomes dense; it is the largest and carries most beats.

- **Chapter Five: First Major Obstacle**
  ◦ Scene: Attempt to control the situation
    ▪ Protagonist acts
    ▪ Something blocks them
    ▪ Stakes rise
  ◦ Scene: Cost is introduced
    ▪ Emotional or practical consequence appears
    ▪ Protagonist reassesses
    ▪ Tension increases

- **Chapter Six: Escalation**
  ◦ Scene: More complications emerge
    ▪ New threats or pressures

- Different areas of life collide
- Opposing force strengthens
- Scene: Protagonist reacts
  - They try to adapt
  - Partial progress
  - A new complication joins
- **Chapter Seven: Alliances and Divisions**
- Scene: Allies appear
  - New support enters the story
  - Relationships begin developing
  - Goals align
- Scene: Opposition surfaces
  - Antagonist or rival gains ground
  - Direct conflict grows
  - Stakes heighten
- **Chapter Eight: Mid-Rising Turning Point**
- Scene: A bold attempt
  - Protagonist tries a risky move
  - Gains brief momentum
  - Hope increases
- Scene: A backlash
  - Attempt triggers a consequence
  - Plans unravel
  - Emotional pressure sharpens
- **Chapter Nine: Approaching Crisis**
- Scene: The problems converge
  - Several conflicts collide
  - Protagonist faces multiple demands
  - Feelings of overwhelm rise
- Scene: A mistake or loss
  - Protagonist misjudges
  - Suffers a setback
  - March toward climax begins
- **Chapter Ten: Final Build**
- Scene: Desperation increases

- Protagonist sees no easy solution
- Conflicts tighten
- Risk escalates
- Scene: Critical decision
  - They choose a path
  - The choice pushes them into the climax
  - Point of no return

III. CLIMAX

(1 chapter, usually 1–2 scenes)

- **Chapter Eleven: The Turning Point**
- Scene: Confrontation
  - Protagonist faces the greatest obstacle
  - All tensions collide
  - The story's highest emotional intensity
- Scene: Outcome is decided
  - Victory, defeat, or transformation
  - Old self meets ultimate test
  - Change (or tragedy) occurs

This is the peak of the entire pyramid.

IV. FALLING ACTION

(2 chapters, 3–5 scenes)

- **Chapter Twelve: Immediate Aftermath**
- Scene: Consequences surface
  - Protagonist processes what happened
  - Supporting cast reacts
  - The world shifts
- Scene: Rebalancing
  - Damage control begins
  - Secondary conflicts resolve
  - Emotional transitions occur

- **Chapter Thirteen: Unraveling the Remaining Threads**
  ◦ Scene: Tension eases
    ▪ Subplots tie up
    ▪ Character relationships realign
    ▪ Practical outcomes clarified
  ◦ Scene: Preparation for closure
    ▪ Show the new emotional landscape
    ▪ Protagonist begins to accept change
    ▪ Resolution begins forming

V. DENOUEMENT

(1 chapter, 1–2 scenes)

- **Chapter Fourteen: Final Resolution**
  ◦ Scene: The new normal
    ▪ Show how the world now functions
    ▪ Demonstrate the protagonist's change
    ▪ Establish stability
  ◦ Scene: Final beat
    ▪ A symbolic or emotional closing moment
    ▪ Reflect on the journey
    ▪ Provide lasting closure

Total Standard Count for Freytag's Pyramid

- 14 chapters
- 20–35 scenes
- 40–80 beats

SEVEN POINT PLOT STRUCTURE — FULL CHAPTER, SCENE, AND BEAT OUTLINE

The Seven-Point Structure consists of:

Hook

First Plot Point

First Pinch Point

Midpoint

Second Pinch Point

Second Plot Point

Resolution

The structure naturally produces **7–10 chapters**, depending on story complexity.
Below is the standard approach.

I. HOOK

(1 chapter, 2–3 scenes)

- **Chapter One: The Character's Starting State**
  ○ Scene: Establish the ordinary world
    ▪ Show daily life
    ▪ Reveal personality and flaw
    ▪ Suggest dissatisfaction or vulnerability
  ○ Scene: Introduce stakes
    ▪ Show what matters to the character
    ▪ Establish relationships
    ▪ Hint at future conflict
  ○ Scene: Foreshadow disruption
    ▪ A small tension appears
    ▪ Tone shifts
    ▪ Uncertainty enters the hero's life

II. FIRST PLOT POINT

(1 chapter, 2 scenes)

- **Chapter Two: The Story Turns**
  - Scene: Major event forces change
    - Disruption hits the character's world
    - They face something unavoidable
    - A new direction becomes necessary
  - Scene: The character crosses into a new situation
    - They make a choice or are pushed
    - Old normal collapses
    - The central conflict becomes clear

III. FIRST PINCH POINT

(1 chapter, 2–3 scenes)

- **Chapter Three: Pressure from the Opposition**
  - Scene: First display of antagonistic force
    - Something threatens the protagonist
    - Opposition is revealed more clearly
    - Fear or tension increases
  - Scene: The cost becomes visible
    - Something valued is put at risk
    - Stakes rise
    - Hero reacts with uncertainty
  - Scene: Movement into struggle
    - Hero attempts first steps
    - They encounter obstacles
    - They realize they are unprepared

IV. MIDPOINT

(1 chapter, 2–3 scenes)

- **Chapter Four: The Big Shift**
  - Scene: Revelation or major discovery
    - Information changes the hero's understanding

- Direction of the story transforms
- Stakes escalate dramatically
- Scene: Hero becomes active instead of reactive
  - They gain confidence or clarity
  - Commit to a course of action
  - Begin taking strategic steps
- Scene: The problem intensifies
  - Victory or defeat reshapes tension
  - Enemy or pressure strengthens
  - The story accelerates

V. SECOND PINCH POINT

(1 chapter, 2–3 scenes)

- **Chapter Five: Heavy Pressure from the Conflict**
- Scene: Antagonist or threat strikes hard
  - A meaningful loss occurs
  - Hero's progress is reversed
  - Stakes hit a painful level
- Scene: Weakness exposed
  - Hero faces internal flaw
  - Their limitations become clear
  - Emotional tension spikes
- Scene: Near breaking point
  - Plans fail
  - Relationships strain
  - Hero inches closer to crisis

VI. SECOND PLOT POINT

(1 chapter, 2–3 scenes)

- **Chapter Six: The Final Piece Appears**
- Scene: Reveal or discovery changes everything
  - Vital information surfaces
  - A missing key becomes known

- The protagonist sees the real path forward
- Scene: Hero prepares for final confrontation
  - Gathers courage, allies, or resources
  - Accepts the theme or inner truth
  - Overcomes denial or fear
- Scene: Final commitment
  - A bold decision or sacrifice is made
  - Hero transitions into the final stretch
  - No turning back

VII. RESOLUTION

(1–2 chapters, 3–5 scenes total)

- **Chapter Seven: The Final Battle**
- Scene: Confrontation with the core problem
  - Hero applies what they learned
  - Climax unfolds
  - Opponent or obstacle is defeated or accepted
- Scene: Outcome becomes clear
  - Hero succeeds or fails
  - Tension releases
  - External conflict resolves

- **Chapter Eight (Optional Standard): New Normal**
- Scene: The world after the struggle
  - Show how life has changed
  - Relationships or roles shift
  - Emotional stability returns
- Scene: Final beat
  - A symbolic action shows new identity
  - Theme becomes clear
  - Story ends with closure

www.ingramcontent.com/pod-product-compliance
Lightning Source LLC
Chambersburg PA
CBHW052129030426

42337CB00028B/5088